Praise for *Magickal Self Defense*

"It is no surprise that a man who has spent the majority of his life defending others would write the definitive book on magickal self-defense. Kerr Cuhulain puts a new face on the old art of magickal warding by presenting us with material backed by quantum theory—the branch of physics that, every day, brings science closer to explaining the magickal arts Pagans have practiced for a long time. Kerr pulls quantum theory down from the lofty bookshelves of the halls of science and breaks it down into fresh and practical concepts anyone can understand and, more importantly, use to protect the body, mind, and spirit. This is a must-have book for anyone who wants to live a life unrestricted by needless fear."

—Edain McCoy, author of *Advanced Witchcraft*
and many other books

"I found Kerr Cuhulain's *Magickal Self Defense* much more than a brilliant book on psychic self-defense. Kerr demystifies psychic self-defense in a clear, no-nonsense approach that invites the reader to deepen in awareness and personal growth. He explains and teaches techniques in the art of being fully present and *response-able*, with implications for magickal practice and daily life. His message demands that we develop ourselves as a tool in our own defense as peaceful warriors in a sometimes dangerous world."

—Ruth Barrett, priestess, musician, and author of
Women's Rites, Women's Mysteries

"A realistic and wonderfully effective approach to defensive magick, Kerr Cuhulain's latest book is a must-read for all of us. Straightforward, easy to understand, and delightfully in-depth, I particularly recommend it for healers, pagan parents, and anyone planning to attend pagan festivals."

—Kristin Madden, author of *The Book of Shamanic Healing*
and *Pagan Parenting*

About the Author

A former Air Force officer, Kerr Cuhulain was a police officer for twenty-nine years and is now a police dispatcher with E-Comm, the emergency communications center for southwestern British Columbia, Canada. He was one of the few publicly Wiccan police officers in the world, serving on a SWAT team, gang crime unit, hostage negotiation team, and a mental health emergency services unit. Kerr is currently the head of Officers of Avalon, an organization representing Pagan professionals who are police officers, firefighters, and paramedics.

Kerr travels throughout North America as a popular speaker at writers' conferences and Pagan festivals, and he has been featured in many books, articles, and media interviews. He is the author of *The Law Enforcement Guide to Wicca*, *Wiccan Warrior*, *Witch Hunts*, and *Full Contact Magick*.

To Write to the Author

If you wish to contact the author or would like more information about this book, please write to the author in care of Llewellyn Worldwide and we will forward your request. Both the author and publisher appreciate hearing from you and learning of your enjoyment of this book and how it has helped you. Llewellyn Worldwide cannot guarantee that every letter written to the author can be answered, but all will be forwarded. Please write to:

Kerr Cuhulain
℅ Llewellyn Worldwide
2143 Wooddale Drive, Dept. 978-0-7387-1219-2
Woodbury, MN 55125-2989, U.S.A.

Please enclose a self-addressed stamped envelope for reply,
or $1.00 to cover costs. If outside the USA, enclose
an international postal reply coupon.

Many of Llewellyn's authors have websites with additional information and resources. For more information, please visit our website at www.llewellyn.com.

A QUANTUM APPROACH TO WARDING

Magickal Self Defense

KERR
CUHULAIN

Llewellyn Publications
Woodbury, Minnesota

First Edition
First Printing, 2008

Book design by Steffani Sawyer
Cover art © 2007 JupiterImages Corporation
Cover design by Lisa Novak
Llewellyn is a registered trademark of Llewellyn Worldwide, Ltd.

Library of Congress Cataloging-in-Publication Data for *Magickal Self Defense: A Quantum Approach to Warding* is on file at the Library of Congress.

ISBN: 978-0-7387-1219-2

Llewellyn Publications
A Division of Llewellyn Worldwide, Ltd.
2143 Wooddale Drive, Dept. 978-0-7387-1219-2
Woodbury, Minnesota 55125-2989, U.S.A.
www.llewellyn.com

Printed in the United States of America

To Selena Fox and her Circle Sanctuary and Lady Liberty League, which have been upholding the rights of Pagans for decades now. Thanks!

Contents

Ward (v.): To avert, repel, or turn aside danger, harm, an attack, or an assailant. From the Middle English *warden*, Old English *weardian*, and German *warden*.

Each time a man stands up for an ideal,
or acts to improve the lot of others,
or strikes out against injustice,
he sends forth a tiny ripple of hope . . .

—Robert F. Kennedy

Introduction

Introduction

Self-defense is nature's oldest law.

—John Dryden

The word *occult* carries plenty of baggage. Since people typically hold negative opinions about that which they don't understand, many in society look askance at the topic of psychic self-defense. Much of the ancient literature on this subject comes from mythology that refers to forces of light arrayed against forces of darkness—such as the Zoroastrian myths and the traditions of occidental ceremonial magick—and even much of the modern literature on this topic is still rooted in myth rather than in science.

Most of the more modern classic texts about psychic self-defense were written in the Newtonian age, before the development of quantum physics gave us a better understanding of both the physical and the psychic worlds. Writers in this classic period of Newtonian physics perceived the universe as a machine, an understanding reflected in disciplines such as occidental ceremonial magick. Many contemporary books on psychic self-defense are based on such old concepts and haven't incorporated modern scientific knowledge. Recent discoveries in the field of quantum mechanics confirm the effectiveness of many old magickal techniques—and then allow us to improve on them. These new discoveries also give us a better understanding of how magick works, providing us with a chance to discard many outdated notions.

You probably think quantum physics is something a bunch of strange people in a laboratory deal with, something you'll never experience. But actually the effects of quantum physics are all around you. For example, every time you watch a supermarket clerk scan an item to record a product's price, you're witnessing a quantum-mechanical event.

The word *quantum* refers to the energy needed for an electron to go from one orbit or state to another. Scientists have discovered that an electron doesn't physically travel between orbits; it simply appears in one or the other without having traveled between the two. One moment an electron is in one orbit, and then suddenly it's in another. From such observations, scientists eventually realized that what we perceive to be "solid" is actually made up of particles that pop in and out of reality from a unified field of infinite potentiality. This infinite potentiality is one of the keys to magick, and you can use it in psychic self-defense.

Quantum mechanics helps us to understand how the universe around us works. If you've been a Pagan for a while, then you've probably encountered all kinds of models meant to explain how the magick you do works. The Witch's Pyramid (a model I'll describe later in this book) and the "cone of power" are typical, everyday examples of such models used widely in Pagan circles. Quantum mechanics is a model being refined constantly as scientists seek out what they call the TOE ("Theory of Everything"), a unified theory of the universe. The latest version is called "M-theory," and it attempts to incorporate five other "string theories" describing elements of quantum mechanics. In this book, I'm going to describe the various basic concepts and elements of this quantum model of the universe that relate to psychic self-defense—and show you how to use them.

One of the oldest concepts in Celtic mythology is the idea that everything is interconnected, just as one of the cornerstones of the science of quantum physics is the concept of entanglement. Again and again, experiments have proved that on the level of the Planck scale, everything *is* connected. One of the implications of this for ancient magickal and mythical concepts is the common idea in older texts on psychic self-defense that any attack that can't reach the subconscious mind will fail. How do we defend ourselves against such an attack, though, if we are all inextricably connected? What implications does all this have for ancient concepts of psychic self-defense? If we are already interconnected, how can we hope to stave off an attack on our subconscious? I will answer these questions for you in this book.

I will be describing a system that relies on the principle that psychic attack and defense aren't about "dominating" as much as they're about:

- Finding the right connection *and*
- Causing the person at the end of that connection to entrain or resonate the way you want them to

Sensing and manipulating the energy and potentiality around you is what psychic self-defense is all about. In this system, your psychic defense utilizes the entrainment of your own vibrations and oscillations, and those of your assailant. In other words, you use the psychic assailant's own energy to defeat them.

Another ancient concept, one of the cornerstones of the systems of Warrior magick that I've described in my earlier books, is the power of one's will. Magick is causing change in conformity with your will. Experiments in modern quantum physics and noetic science have confirmed the effects of will: The observer affects what is observed. You perceive what you *expect* to perceive.

This book will show you that intention is one of the keys to success in psychic self-defense. Psychic defense often comes down to the person who has the strongest will.

Experiments in modern quantum physics also show us that time is flexible. In quantum mechanics, this is called *time-reversal symmetry*. Time can be experienced both backward and forward. Affecting things that happened earlier in time is an essential element of psychic self-defense. If you start to react once the attack has commenced, it will already be too late: the connection has been activated and all you can do is shut part of it out. An important part of developing psychic-safety awareness is cultivating the ability to reach backward in time to sense a possible threat. I'll discuss this in more depth later in this book.

There's an old saying: "If you believe you are hexed, you are." I get countless e-mails from individuals who think their misfortunes, bad luck, and setbacks can be blamed on psychic attacks by others. In many cases, I find that this isn't so at all. Instead, most of the drama is caused by the person perceiving it. The average person isn't constantly awash in negative energy nor are they constantly being attacked by ghosts, sorcerers, or creatures of darkness. I'm rarely under attack, and it's a sure bet that you aren't either. Road rage is a bigger threat to the average person than psychic attacks.

However, it is true that every day each and every one of us is exposed to stress, other people's emotional baggage, and various environmental factors. These stressors account for over 90 percent of what people perceive to be psychic attacks, and this negative energy is probably responsible for many of the neuroses and illnesses we see in our daily lives. (Only about 10 percent of the negative influences we experience in our lives comes from what some authors refer to as "metaphysical sources."[1]) This book will show you how to deal with all this other negative energy, too.

---

1. Dr. Bruce Goldberg, "Psychic Self Defense," http://www.drbrucegoldberg.com/defense.htm (accessed 12 February 2007).

This book doesn't offer a cure for paranoia. People suffering from paranoia believe that they're constantly being stalked, watched, or attacked. Paranoia is a symptom of some mental disorders and of the long-term use of street drugs. Having worked for nine years in the mental-health emergency services unit of a major police department, and later as a police dispatcher, I've seen countless examples of this paranoia. These unfortunates are unable to identify their "assailants" except in very vague terms. That's because these assailants don't exist.

If this sounds familiar, you should consider consulting a mental-health professional. No one deserves to live in constant anxiety, especially when it is preventable, as this sort of paranoia is. Most paranoia and psychosis is easily treated, and such treatment is nothing to be ashamed of. Movies like *A Beautiful Mind* demonstrate that people suffering from such mental disorders can live normal lives and achieve great things.

So how can you tell the difference between real psychic attack and mental illness? As a general rule, a key symptom is obsession: if the symptoms that you perceive are due to a mental illness, nothing you do except for a medical intervention will make the perceived attacks go away. And that's because the actual problem is not being addressed.

If you use street drugs such as crack cocaine or crystal methamphetamine, you *will* develop paranoia. You will *very likely* develop symptoms that will give you the impression you're under psychic attack. If you're in this situation, put this book down now, seek professional medical help, and enter a drug-rehabilitation program. It's not a psychic attack you're experiencing, but rather the symptoms of the damage you're inflicting on your brain. I hope that if you are in this situation, you will still have enough insight after reading this to seek help. If not, I hope you have loyal friends or family members who will intervene to save you. Otherwise your outlook is extremely bleak.

If you believe that things in your life will go wrong, they usually will; such beliefs are a negative way of creating your own reality. Believing that someone has the power to do psychic damage to you will amplify that intent and often give the other person such an ability. If you think you're surrounded by idiots in need of correction, you're going to invite challenges into your life.

The theatrical traditions surrounding Shakespeare's play *Macbeth* are a good example of this process. Many stage performers believe that *Macbeth* is "jinxed." They won't even utter the name "Macbeth" when referring to it; instead, they call it as the "Scottish play." My wife and I were once called in to a local theatre company to show them how to overcome this belief system and defuse this ticking time bomb of belief. The play went ahead without incident.

Often, people who want me to protect them against psychic attacks or negative energy tell me they have consulted a legion of "occult experts" and healers before coming to me. They've spent lots of time and money trying to get others to build up some sort of magickal defenses for them. But often these defenses, if they work at all, only work for a short time. They eventually erode as their energy is depleted, like a battery running down. A better option is to develop your personal magickal skills to deal with these situations instead of relying on others to apply band-aid cures. You can defend yourself, and this book will show you how. It will also show you how to find your strengths, and use them effectively to empower yourself without inviting negative energy into your life.

If you've already got some magickal training, this book will, I hope, give you a different perspective and some new ideas to make your training more effective. If you haven't already had any magickal training, this book will provide you with the basics you need to establish the wards necessary to defend yourself from the chaotic world out there.

Psychic Attacks

ONE

Psychic Attacks

*All I'm trying to do is
not join my ancestral spirits just yet.*

—Joshua Nkomo

A true "psychic attack" occurs when a person deliberately projects a clearly defined malicious intent upon someone else. This attack may affect the victim's mental state, causing stress, anxiety, and sleeplessness. This in turn affects the victim's physical body, causing disease and, in extremely rare cases, even death, because the attack is affecting the victim's nonphysical energy field. Psychic attacks range from short, sharp, highly emotionally charged onslaughts linked with a clear desire for negative consequences to extended, elaborate, rituals of negative magick. Whichever is used by the assailant, the principles of psychic self-defense are the same.

I've heard many people advance the argument that "the ancient warriors knew that any purely defensive battle is doomed, if it goes on long enough."[2] Usually this is a lead-

2. Jordsvin, "Basic Magickal Protection & Psychic Self-Defense," http://www.wicca.com/celtic/wicca/defense.htm (accessed 12 February 2007).

in to an argument that "the best defense is offense." Psychic self-defense books and articles are full of examples of psychic attack techniques.

During my twenty-nine years as a police officer, I learned how to defend myself and others without becoming aggressive. This was essential, as police officers are criminally liable for any excessive force that they use. The insights that I gained from this experience, combined with my thirty-nine years as a Pagan as well as my martial arts experience helped me to develop strategies that are as effective in psychic self-defense as they are in physical self-defense. You don't need to attack in order to defend yourself from psychic attacks.

In the physical world the Warrior avoids getting into battles. The Chinese general Sun Tzu taught us that "those who win every battle are not really skillful—those who render others' armies helpless without fighting are the best of all."[3] I don't want you to get into a psychic battle. Nor do I want you to enter into a protracted cycle of attack and counterattack between you and some cretin who doesn't like you. I want you to win without going to war. Sending your own negative energy at your assailant can certainly affect them. Unfortunately, the effect often includes motivating the assailant to retaliate. The techniques that I will show you in this book are assertive without being aggressive. They will shut down the assailant's attack and hopefully leave them unwilling and probably unable to attack you again.

Ormungandr, writing from his perspective as an Ásatrúar, put it this way:

> *Psychic Self-defense is not about being isolationist or being afraid of the world. Nor is it making what we feel or think*

---

3. Sun Tzu (trans. by Thomas Cleary), *The Art of War* (Boston: Shambhala, 1991), 18.

someone else's responsibility. It is definitely not for engaging in psychic warfare. It is totally non-violent, non-judgmental, non-projective or implosive. It is about self-knowledge, self-sovereignty and "owning" our being as a sacred spiritual place.[4]

As I pointed out in my earlier books, being a Warrior is not about using your hands; it is about using your head. It's about taking charge of your life. We can find examples of this concept in all places and ages. Let's look at some examples:

· In the fifth century BCE, the Greek historian Herodotus said that "where wisdom is called for, force is of little use."

· In the final ritual of the Masai manhood ritual, the senior tribal elders encourage the graduates to "drop your weapons and use your head and wisdom instead."[5]

· In the seventeenth century CE, the Samurai philosopher Miyamoto Musashi wrote that the "trained martial artist . . . truly acts only in response to aggression. He does not seek it out. When made, his responses are nonresistant and nonviolent. He is a man of peace."[6]

Christopher Penczak advocates "compassionate defense" in his book *The Witch's Shield*:

When you send harmful energy away, realize that there is no "away." When you sever an unhealthy connection, you are still connected. We are all one in our uniqueness and diversity. Instead of severing, cutting away, isolating, or blocking the experience, seek to heal it. . . . It is easy to label the enemy

---

4. Ormungandr, "Spirit of Yggdrasil," http://www.spirit-of-yggdrasil.com/ page346.aspx (accessed 18 October 2006).

5. Carol Beckwith and Angela Fisher, "Masai Passage to Manhood," *National Geographic* magazine, vol. 196, no. 3 (September 1999), 65.

6. Miyamoto Musashi, *The Book of Five Rings* (New York: Bantam, 1988), xxvii.

as evil, but when we rise above the ego, we often realize that things are not as cut and dried as simple good and evil.[7]

Again, this book isn't about being aggressive. It is about being assertive. There is nothing wrong with assertiveness if it comes from your center, without a desire to appear strong or make the other person appear wrong. Power doesn't come from accumulating energy and/or defenses. True power comes from mastering your situation. Master yourself, and everything else in your life will take care of itself.

Part of taking charge of your life is taking responsibility for your life. As I mentioned in the introduction to this book, people have a very bad habit of seeking excuses for the problems in their lives. Instead of recognizing that they've made a mistake or brought about an uncomfortable situation through their neglect or carelessness, they seek to find someone else to blame. They'd like to park the blame in the lap of some trickster god, some nasty elemental force of nature, or even fate. Many people try to attribute their misfortune to psychic attacks. Our misfortunes are often our own fault. The Wiccan Rede and the Nine Noble Virtues of Ásatrú teach us to take responsibility for our actions. Before you blame your misfortunes on a "psychic attack," take a close look at yourself. It could be that you are the author of your own misfortunes.

The psychic attack situations (both real and imagined) that I've encountered over the years fit into one of four categories:

1: Local influences
The individual having problems may be located in an area where elemental forces are concentrated. Checking the local geography and consulting a map for nearby sites of power

---

7. Christopher Penczak, *The Witch's Shield: Protection Magick & Psychic Self-Defense* (St. Paul, MN: Llewellyn, 2004), 101–102.

often reveals the source of the problem. Sensitivity to your surroundings forms the basis for psychometry and divination. If you haven't trained yourself to deal with this sensitivity, it can cause problems for you. Natural or elemental forces are not "evil," but they can exert a powerful influence on you.

Another possibility is that what you may be experiencing is leftover residue from novice or unskilled occultists in your area who are not grounding their energies properly after ritual. This is a possibility if rituals or magick were recently conducted at the location that is causing you the problems. I will speak about grounding such surplus energy in a later chapter.

The immediate effects of the energy field of such a location or object can be felt within twelve to thirty feet of its location. Lesser effects can be experienced out to between 100 to 300 yards from such objects, depending on your sensitivity. If your sensitivity to the location is the problem, then avoiding elemental areas such as ley lines or power centers may help, at least until you've learned how to deal with them. Urban dwellers often find that cities can create a "buffer" for elemental energy like this, but it comes at the cost of becoming disconnected from powerful elemental forces that can be of great help to Pagans practicing magick. This is a problem if you are trying to connect to elemental energy, but can provide some protection to those who are overly sensitive.

If you are sensitive to the energy around you, then places where human suffering has occurred are locations for you to avoid. The problem should resolve itself if you remove yourself from the influence of the location or item involved. The negative energy created by dramatic events dissipates slowly. The more traumatic the event, the longer its effects will linger in an area. Sensitive people in the vicinity will become aware of it in some way or another. For example, most people who visit the

Auschwitz death camp can still feel the suffering of the people who were murdered there.

Examples of places with negative energy include casinos, sleazy pubs, family and bankruptcy courts, and criminal hangouts. I sense a quiet desperation around such places. You may be sensitive to the nasty energy of constantly quarreling neighbors (especially in apartment buildings or condominiums). The anxiety surrounding the psychiatric wards of hospitals can also have a strong effect. If you must go to such places, keep your barriers up. As I've mentioned, my experience working the mental-health emergency services car for my police department gave me some experience with this.

This negative energy can be detected in all kinds of common things in our everyday lives. Who made the clothes you are wearing, the house you live in, or the car you drive? What were these people thinking or experiencing when they made these things for your use? Were they manufactured by depressed, disgruntled, and impoverished people working in appalling factory conditions? Were some of those workers alcoholics or drug addicts? Did some of them leave work, go home, commit acts of violence on their wife and children, and build your car the next morning? Everything that we come into contact with can hold some of the thought energy of those who were in contact with it before you. If you are overly sensitive to such psychometric energy, then this can have a negative effect on you.

Negative energy can accumulate in a household, but there are many ways to deal with it. A clean and orderly house allows the energy or chi to flow properly and does not let negative energy accumulate. Negative thought-forms accumulate in messy environments. Squalor leads to depression. Physical garbage attracts psychic garbage. Messy environments resonate with the chaos represented by such disorganized states. An organized household fosters an organized mind. An organized mind is much more capable of defense than a disorganized mind. You do more than just emptying the garbage pail when you take out the trash.

Another possibility for sensitive people is the presence of curios, paraphernalia, or items once used in magick. Having these objects in your vicinity may cause adverse effects. Of course, if you really are under psychic attack, there is a possibility that such magickal objects were deliberately left there. Objects in your vicinity that are unfamiliar are suspect. This is talismanic magick, a very old technique. The idea is that the object left in your vicinity will help to create a link with you through which your assailant can focus the attack. A talisman of some sort is made and then brought into contact with the victim. It may be placed in your house or a room that you frequent. It may be placed in your yard or buried in a path that you frequently use in your everyday work. I'll explain in more detail in chapter 11 about how to deal with talismans and amulets used as links or point d'appui.

2: Human influences

By human influences I mean people directing negative forces at the victim. This isn't always a conscious process. Deliberate psychic attacks are a comparatively *rare* occurrence. Even when they can be traced back to an individual, in most cases such "attacks" are unconscious: the "psychic assailant," while possibly aware of their ill feelings toward you, is actually unaware that they are sending negative energy and influences at you. There are many negative people out there, and some of them may have it in for you. Most of these people have no training in any magickal disciplines. They simply have a natural talent that allows them to project their negativity in your direction. Keith Randolph, in his article "Psychic Self Defense," observes that " . . . fierce, concentrated anger can trigger malevolent psychokinesis or bring an evil elemental into the picture, even if the human agent doesn't know that such things are possible."[8] On rare occasions there may be bonds between victim and assailant from past incarnations that facilitate a negative energy transfer between individuals.

The "psychic attack" that you perceive might be the energy thrown at you by extremists in your neighborhood fervently praying for the salvation of your soul. This could be an unconscious attempt to impose their will on you or a deliberate attempt to force you into the pews of their church by any means necessary. Many Pagans of my acquaintance would consider that negative magick. Fortunately most people in revealed religions such as Christianity and Islam are inclined to put out positive energy, not hateful energy.

One must consider the aggressor's desires and their motives for attacking you. The aggressor's perception of you or of their situation may be flawed. The aggressor's anxieties may have no basis in reality. This is especially true if these anxieties arise from mental illness. Of course, real or not, this may not prevent the aggressor from feeling justified in initiating an attack. Of course, this flawed perception of the assailant may also make it difficult for you to identify them, as it may not be a perception that you are aware of. As the perceptions of the aggressor and victim can differ, the victim may have no understanding of the motives or scale of an unprovoked psychic attack. This is where it is important to let go and let your intuition guide you. I'll have more to say about intuition and threat awareness in the next chapter.

---

8. Keith Randolph, "Psychic Self Defense," The Llewellyn Encyclopedia, http://www.llewellynencyclopedia.com/article/271 (accessed 13 February 2007).

3: Overextension

Overextension occurs when the victim has ventured beyond their capabilities in magick. Overextending yourself leads to problems. There is an old magickal adage: don't open the door unless you know how to close (and lock) it. When instinct is at work, we experience emotional energy. Those new to New Age or Pagan pursuits often find themselves experiencing new things. These new experiences can often lead to unfamiliar feelings. Magickal training increases levels of sensitivity, which in turn makes you more susceptible to energy and emotions in your vicinity. The more experience you acquire, the more you will become aware of the previously undetected energy of others surrounding you. This might feel like a psychic attack to the uninitiated.

People attend Pagan festivals for various reasons. Some go to such gatherings in order to socialize, some to learn, some just to drum and dance. A lot of random energy is being generated at Pagan gatherings. Think of this random energy as white noise or static. Some of the people creating this energy are new and/or untrained and not at all capable of controlling their personal energy. Even those who are trained sometimes forget about grounding and warding until something negative happens. When you are in close proximity to others, you will exchange energy with them unless you've done something to prevent this exchange. Direct contact such as hugs or handshaking enhances energy exchange. Such intimate activity usually occurs between people who care for one another, and you know the pleasant feelings such positive energy exchange can bring. You've probably also experienced the unpleasant feelings that surround people who are disagreeable or negative. If the person you are in contact with has negative energy, then such contact may not be a good thing.

When you first attend large Pagan gatherings, you may get "psychic indigestion" from energy you are unused to. Pagan author Patricia Telesco warns that "as you begin to attend festivals you'll also start to notice that there's a lot of psychological and spiritual drama that occurs at these events . . . typically in the last day or two of the gathering."[9] Typical symptoms of this "overload" can include:

- headache
- nightmares
- insomnia
- anxiety

It is important to be aware of your health, energy levels, and emotional states at such gatherings.

4: Health problems

Health problems may occur when the victim is suffering from a pathological condition which opens their "aura," allowing negative influences to get in. As I mentioned earlier, health problems can also occur when the victim is suffering from a mental disorder that gives them the false impression that they are under psychic attack.

At the outset of any investigation into a perceived psychic attack, one should always eliminate the possibility of psychosis and/or delirium due to a medical condition. Strong emotions such as fear can become conduits for negative energy. Drunks and addicts attract such energy. In turn they can exude a negative energetic atmosphere that affects all those around them. This can lead to paranoia and fear. The paranoid victim starts hurling magickal thunderbolts at all manner of imagined

---

9. Patricia Telesco, "Psychic Self Defense For Festivals (and Beyond)," 28 August 2002, http://www.witchvox.com/va/dt_va.html?a=usny&c=festtips&id=4661 (accessed 17 October 2007).

threats, which invariably causes even greater problems. The whole subject of "psychic protection" needs to be approached with caution.

At one time or other, everybody experiences one of these four situations. Keep these four scenarios in mind when you are trying to identify the source of the unpleasant energy you may be experiencing.

The psychic attacks that I will be teaching you to defend yourself against originate in the second category: human influences. As I pointed out, these psychic assaults can take the form of an overt attack from someone who is angry with you. They can take a more subtle and insidious form when somebody silently and secretly sends you negative thoughts and emotions or ill will, whether they are aware of it or not.

Negative psychic energy can "contaminate" you. It can deplete your energy. It can cause you mental, emotional, and physical distress. This, in turn, can prevent you from achieving your aims and objectives. Psychic attacks can cause physical, emotional, and mental disease. Later in this book I will teach you techniques to protect yourself against such attacks. Also, in a later chapter I will go into more detail about how your health affects your ability to defend yourself.

Negative energy is not something to be ignored. As you can see from the list of four influences above, there is a lot of negative and chaotic energy in the world around you, and it can affect you adversely if you aren't cautious. It is certainly possible to harm another person with magick. If you do nothing but sit and dwell on your concerns, you'll only make them worse. You need to take responsibility for your life. But I'm not urging you to become obsessive about defending yourself from negative energy. Psychic self-defense is about finding a way to balance the energy around you to lead a healthy, happy life.

Fear is what allows destructive magick to get a hold on you. Destructive magick can't work on you effectively if you don't fear it. Sometimes the lack of fear renders magickal attacks utterly impotent. To deal with psychic attacks you need to learn techniques like those listed in this book. The difficulty is that until you learn these skills, you will likely lack the confidence to use these defense techniques effectively. People fear the unknown.

To help the beginner deal with this, I am first going to teach you some simple techniques that you can use until you have developed sufficient power and confidence to do without them. You can think of these techniques as a form of armor, like the body armor a police officer wears on patrol. Armor can be overcome, but it does provide a level of protection against the consequences of the unexpected.

Later I will show you an approach to psychic self-defense that is based on using the attacker against himself. Those of you who have studied martial arts will recognize this approach, which forms the basis of push-pull techniques in Japanese arts like Aikido or Jujitsu and the hubud techniques in Escrima. I'll show you how to redirect destructive energy directed at you back into the universal pool from which all energy comes.

Symptoms of Psychic Attack

Recognizing the symptoms is the first step in overcoming psychic attacks. The symptoms of a psychic attack vary from one individual to another. Symptoms include, but are not limited to, the following:

- A feeling of weight pressing down on you while you are asleep or dreaming
- Continuous and intensifying sense of oppression or fear while awake

- Nervous exhaustion or wasting away when there is no medically diagnosable physical cause
- Repetitive nightmares, which may ultimately make the sufferer reluctant to sleep. These nightmares may have themes such as:
  › Being chased or assaulted
  › Being confronted by some person or agency that feels somehow external to you
  › Forecasts of doom
  › A sense of foreboding
- A sense of being watched or stalked when there is no one around
- Physical manifestations, including in extreme cases:
  › Bruises
  › Obnoxious odors that come and go with no apparent physical cause. (These odors will be noticed by anyone who is around when they are present.)
  › Auditory effects: bell, snaps, clicks—often indicating something trying to manifest physically
  › Poltergeists
  › Fires
- Fear and/or feelings of isolation
- The intuitive or visible presence of a manifest thought-form or simulacrum (more on this later)
- An inexplicable numbing, followed by paralysis, beginning at the feet and extending gradually up the body
- Jabbing or prickling sensations, typically in the hands, feet, lower legs, or back
- Rapid onset of constant choking or a feeling of suffocation with no apparent causes

A real psychic attack is usually associated with a person or relationship. If you start experiencing any of the symptoms above, the next thing you need to do is identify the source. There will be some sort of motivation that can be discerned in the details. People don't usually consciously engage in psychic attacks unless they have a strong motivation: conscious psychic attacks are hard work. People don't normally engage in such activity for trivial reasons. If the psychic assailant is unconsciously sending negative energy at you, it should still be possible to identify the assailant's emotions and feelings that are fueling the psychic assault.

You need to pay attention to these symptoms. Psychic attack can lead to a negative state of mind and/or depression. Depression, in turn, can weaken your defenses. Emotional, sexual, or magickal intimacy with others under attack can transfer some of the negativity from the victim to those around them. Negative emotions like rage and anger can create and attract negative energy. Thus it is important to recognize these symptoms and to take action in a timely fashion.

So far I've discussed the sources of negative energy and the symptoms of psychic attack. In the next chapter I will show you how to develop the safety awareness that will help you to identify the source and nature of such attacks.

Psychic Threat Awareness

two

Psychic Threat Awareness

Reality is that which, when you stop believing in it,
doesn't go away.

—Philip K. Dick

You *can* defend yourself against psychic attack. It is very important for you to understand this. However, in light of what I showed you in the last chapter, you can see that in order to do so you must first be able to correctly identify such attacks and determine their source.

As I mentioned earlier, most of the classic texts on psychic self-defense come from an age of classic physics, in which the world was viewed as a machine. One of the most important consequences of the discovery of quantum physics is that we can no longer view the world this way. The universe must be viewed as an organism, and this is a worldview akin to many Pagan spiritual beliefs. This awareness of the universe around you as an interconnected organism is exactly what I want you to use to better defend yourself.

Threat awareness is the first step in protection. Safety involves an ongoing assessment of the possible threats around you. This is not a matter of paranoia. I don't want you to get anxious about possible threats. I just want you to maintain a proper awareness of what is happening around you. Doing so creates a filter around you that will bring to your attention anything that might do harm to you, which, in turn, allows you to react appropriately. This is basically just focused intuition. A little understanding of the enemy can save you a lot of hard work and worries. You need to try to understand the way your assailant thinks and what his objectives may be in order for your defenses to be effective. Awareness gives you that information.

You must learn to trust your intuition. We *all* have psychic abilities, but most of us have let these skills lie dormant. I saw examples of this all the time when I was a cop: I ran into countless police officers who have experienced what they may call hunches, premonitions, intuitions, or gut feelings all the time. If only most of them acted on these psychic impulses. Most people in Western society (especially cops) are extremely reluctant to admit to any but a few close friends (if at all) that they have such psychic flashes. Certainly most cops who experience such premonitions explain this phenomenon away as anything but magickal. Yet these abilities are the birthright of everyone on this planet.

Part of the problem in developing psychic awareness comes from how your perceptions are created. Your brain takes in four billion bits of information per second. Normally it only pays attention to about two thousand bits.[10] That leaves a lot of room for improvement in the awareness department.

To further complicate things, human beings, in their normal cognitive state, have a limited capacity for attention. For example, driving on the freeway you are only peripherally aware of your friend's conversation in the backseat or the pedestrians

---

10. Dr. Joseph Dispenza, DC, in *What the Bleep!?: Down the Rabbit Hole*, DVD, directed by William Arntz and Betsy Chasse (2006; Los Angeles: 20th Century Fox Home Entertainment).

walking by on adjacent sidewalks. As you work at your computer, the room details and sounds of the dwelling around you fade away. As you become more and more focused, you may even be startled when a family member or co-worker enters the room you're working in.

To be effective in psychic self-defense, you must become more aware of what is going on around you. You must cultivate awareness. You must learn to be constantly aware of your own feelings and intuitions. You must learn to use all of your senses to keep track of what is going on around you. This is something that I always tried to teach my police recruits. If something "feels" out of place, examine it and act upon it immediately. By the time logic and conscious awareness engage, precious time has elapsed. It is far better to trust your intuition and be wrong than to wait for conscious awareness and be trapped. You may be surprised to learn how often your intuitions turn out to be right.

The trick is to set up this awareness as a "body memory," as they say in martial arts circles. Before I become consciously aware of a threat, I feel the hair standing up on the back of my neck. I feel the chi start to flow outward as my wards activate, automatically going from "standby" to maximum power. This happens before I am consciously aware of the threat. Feeling the wards activate is sometimes my first conscious indication that my subconscious has detected a threat.

Awareness encompasses the ability to anticipate threats. One of the discoveries in quantum physics that can assist us in this regard is the flexibility of time.

It was Sir Isaac Newton who gave us the first mathematical model for time, in his *Principia Mathematica* in 1687. In Newtonian physics, time and space are a background in which events take place. Time in Newton's world is like a single line railroad track running in one direction. It is fixed and inflexible, an ever-rolling stream that bears our dreams away, as the old biblical hymn says. Time was considered eternal, having always existed.

Then, in 1905, along came Albert Einstein and his concept of relativity. Einstein realized that the laws of nature should appear the same to all freely moving observers. Only relative motion was relevant. This meant that there was no such thing as absolute rest, as was believed in the old Newtonian system. It also meant that there was no universal time that all clocks could measure. Physicist and author Stephen Hawking tells us: "Einstein's theory of relativity transformed space and time from a passive background in which events take place to active participants in the dynamics of the universe."[11] Einstein combined time with the dimensions of space to create the new concept of space-time. It can be shown that the gravitational effects of matter and energy in the universe warp and distort space-time. There were a lot of other implications beyond this, such as Einstein's famous equation relating mass, energy, and velocity, which gave us the ultimate speed of light and the atomic bomb. Relativity tells us that space-time is curved, not flat and linear as it was held to be in the old Newtonian view of the universe. It is the time portion of this relativity that I want to focus on right now though.

Have you ever thought about how a baseball player hits a ball coming at him at a hundred miles per hour? Scientists have calculated that the time it takes for the batter to see the pitch, decide how to swing, and then actually make the swing takes longer than it takes for the ball to go from pitcher to catcher.[12] How then is it possible for the batter to hit the ball?

---

11. Stephen Hawking, *The Universe in a Nutshell* (New York: Bantam, 2001), 21.

12. Stuart Hameroff, MD, in *What the Bleep!?: Down the Rabbit Hole* (DVD, 2006). Dr. Hameroff is a professor of anesthesiology and psychology studies, associate director for the Center for Consciousness, and an anesthesiologist at the University of Arizona Medical Center.

Is the batter's mind reaching back in time to make the decision? Experiments in modern quantum physics show that time can be experienced backward or forward. Experiments in noetic science based on these theories show us that the idea of the batter reaching back in time with his mind is a very real possibility.

In the late 1970s, neurophysiologist Benjamin Libet conducted experiments on patients undergoing brain surgery. He applied a stimulus to the patient's finger and measured the response time in their brain. He then stimulated the brain to determine how long it would take for the patient to feel this stimulus in their finger. Logic would seem to tell us that if the brain was stimulated, the finger should "feel" an immediate response and that if the finger is stimulated there should be a delay as the signal travels to the brain. This is not the case. Libet proved that *exactly the opposite occurs*. The results of Libet's experiments can be found in his book *Mind Time: The Temporal Factor in Consciousness*.[13] Other researchers have since replicated this experiment, on one occasion with earthworms.

"There's a line of research which considers the brain as an anticipatory system, which means that a lot of what our brain is engaged in is trying to figure out what's coming next," says Dr. Dean Radin, a researcher studying quantum effects as they relate to psychic abilities. " . . . Our brain is always unconsciously scanning for potential danger and for other possibilities. This anticipatory processing means that a large chunk of our cognitive processing is devoted to figuring out probabili-

---

13. Benjamin Libet and Stephen M. Kosslyn, *Mind Time: The Temporal Factor in Consciousness* (Cambridge, MA: Harvard University Press, 2004). Republished online at "Libet's Short Delay," http://www.consciousentities .com/libet.htm (accessed 26 March 2007).

ties of future events."[14] Part of this process is evidently reaching back in time with our minds.

Another experiment conducted by Dean Radin, Dick Berman, and others involves showing people randomly generated emotional images to elicit strong or calm responses and timing the galvanic skin, respiration, and heart rate response.[15] The response occurred a half second to two seconds *before* the image appeared on the screen. Two other researchers have since replicated this over four hundred trials.

One key experiment by Radin involved making an audio tape of binary zeros and ones with a computer random generator.[16] A copy of this tape was made and put in a vault. The volunteer subjects of the experiment were asked to focus on the completed binary tape to make it have more ones than zeros *without listening to it*. Not only did the tape that the subjects focused upon have more ones after they focused their attention on it, *but the copy in the vault that the subjects had never seen was found to be identical to the tape that the subjects focused on*. This experiment has been replicated again and again. The only possible explanation is that the subjects are reaching back in time to influence the tape at the time that it was generated.

We only experience Newtonian time in our normal consciousness. The second law of thermodynamics tells us that things run down over time: this is called entropy. However, quantum mechanics proves that reality is quite different. Quantum mechanics tells us that there is what scientists refer to as a time-reversal symmetry in the universe. Time can be

---

14. Dean Radin, PhD, "Interview With Dean Radin, Part I, The Bleeping Herald," vol. 2, issue 1 (April 2006), http://www.whatthebleep.com/herald12/radin6.shtml.

15. Dean Radin, PhD, in *What the Bleep!?: Down the Rabbit Hole* (DVD, 2006).

16. Ibid.

experienced both forward *and* backward. Quantum researchers such as Kip Thorne[17] and David Deutsch[18] now postulate multiple parallel universes and the possibility of time travel.

This ability to experience time in both directions is an important ability to cultivate and attend to. Detecting events that happened earlier in time is a key to psychic defense. Like the baseball batter or the martial artist sparring in the dojo, you can develop the ability to reach back a bit in time to give yourself the edge in a defensive situation. The only difference in this situation is that you aren't striking out physically at your attacker. As it is a psychic attack, you are reacting mentally. As I pointed out earlier, if you start to react once the attack has commenced it is already too late: the connection has been made and all you can do is shut part of it out. Developing your ability to reach back in time a bit allows you the early warning that you need to shut the psychic "door" in your attacker's face. Part of developing safety awareness is developing the ability to reach backward to sense a possible threat.

Habits, Routines, and Vulnerability

Part of developing safety awareness is becoming aware of your habits. Habits and routines in your life may leave you vulnerable. This is something that I learned early on in my police career. Frequenting particular coffee shops and restaurants will sooner or later come to the attention of the people who wish you harm. You're setting yourself up for an ambush. As I've pointed out in my earlier books, a Warrior has no routines. A Warrior is, as Don Juan so aptly put it, "unavailable." You

---

17. Stephen Hawking, *The Universe in a Nutshell*, 133–153.

18. David Deutsch, "The Physics of David Deutsch," http://www.geocities .com/iona_m/Cosmology/DeutschPhysics.html (accessed 17 October 2007).

don't want to become a creature of habit. You want to be fluid, spontaneous, and elusive.

There are some routines in your life over which you have little control. Your employer probably sets your work schedule. If you must work nine to five, Monday to Friday, there isn't much that you can do to alter that. Most people have a fixed address. I'm not suggesting that you improve your psychic safety by becoming a nomad. You may have a favorite café or coffee shop. Most of us aren't cops who need to be concerned about congregating at such places regularly.

However, there are plenty of habits and routines in our lives over which we have quite a lot of control. As I said, routines and habits can set you up to be ambushed. A Warrior should avoid routines and remain spontaneous and fluid. This does not mean that routines and regimens don't have their place. It means that you should not allow yourself to be fettered by them: routines shouldn't prevent flexibility and innovation. They shouldn't be a liability. If a change is called for, you should not hesitate to change. Bruce Lee put it this way: "The classical man is just a bundle of routine, ideas, and tradition. When he acts, he is translating every living moment in terms of the old."[19]

If you must always walk or drive the same route or you must always meet for coffee at the same coffee shop, don't let the familiarity of the situation lull you into a state of complacency and inattention. Be aware of what is going on around you. Keep your wits about you.

Habits and routines make people comfortable. This comfort can give you the illusion of security. Routines make it look as if we are in control of our situation. Letting go of habits can feel like a loss of control in your life. In reality, letting go of habits will lead to even greater power. Claiming that you must be

---

19. Bruce Lee, *Tao of Jeet Kune Do* (Santa Clarita, CA: Ohara Publications, 1975), 16.

under "psychic attack" to explain away problems that you have caused yourself is simply another aspect of such illusions. If you want to be in control, you need to own your actions and take charge of your life. Overcoming your weaknesses takes a lot of courage. Act the way you'd like to be, and soon you'll be the way you act.

True control over your situation means identifying and taking responsibility for habits that may become problems in your life. Our actions should be influenced by our awareness, not by routines. Each of our acts should have a meaning. As I pointed out in my book *Full Contact Magick*, our lives should be defined by intent, not fate. Habits and addictions are compulsive behaviors that leave us vulnerable. The Wiccan Rede commences with the words "An it harm none . . . " *None* includes you.

Safety stems from simple principles. One of the simplest ways to enhance your security is to eliminate habits and routines in your life. This simple measure will give you a strong foundation from which you can further protect yourself.

Developing awareness can come from long hours in the martial arts arena or sports field, but it can also be developed through quite simple meditation exercises. These exercises will be the focus of the next chapter.

To Know and to Keep Silent

THREE

To Know and to Keep Silent

Hold every moment sacred. Give each clarity and meaning, each the weight of thine awareness, each its true and due fulfillment.

—Thomas Mann, *The Beloved Returns*, 1939

In my earlier books *Wiccan Warrior* and *Full Contact Magick*, I discussed a magickal model created by Clifford Bias in *The Ritual Book of Magic* and modified by Amber K's book *True Magic*: the Witch's Pyramid. In this book I'm going to introduce you to a model of magick that uses the same principles as the Witch's Pyramid but describes them in a manner more suited to psychic self-defense: Magickal Artillery. Magickal Artillery is simply a model, like quantum mechanics, that one can use to describe a system, in this case a system of magick. Magickal Artillery is a model that helps us to understand the interaction of five important magickal principles:

"To Know, To Keep Silent, To Dare, To Imagine, To Will."

In magick, these five principles or axioms interact together to form a functioning whole. If any one of these principles is missing or flawed, the magickal energy will either fail to travel to its target or not have the desired effect. The object is to develop each of the five elements of Magickal Artillery in order to master them and your magick.

Magickal Artillery is like a gun or a howitzer that shoots magick. To Know is the base from which your magick is launched. It is your fire base, if you will. To Keep Silent means scanning your environment to identify any threats that need to be dealt with. It is like your personal radar, seeking out intruders. To Dare is loading yourself up with the psychic defensive charge that you want to send out. It is the magickal "ammunition." To Imagine is setting your sights on the target of your magick. To Will is pulling the trigger and letting the magick fly, steering it into its target like a cruise missile.

In the previous chapter I discussed the importance of developing your awareness and of utilizing the flexibility and relativity of time. In this chapter I want to show you how to train your mind to expand your awareness to enhance your abilities in psychic self-defense. To do this, I'm going to focus on the first two principles of Magickal Artillery: To Know and To Keep Silent.

To Know

Awareness is to Know. It is the base for your Magickal Artillery, the platform from which your defensive magick is launched. I have called it "To Know" rather than "knowledge" for a good reason. The term *knowing*, as I use it, is a process the ancient Greeks called *gnosis*, which means "knowing on a deep psychological and spiritual level." It isn't an accumulation of bits of knowledge; it is active awareness. Knowing is a dynamic process. As author Dan Millman once said: "Understanding is one-dimensional.... Realization, on the other hand, is three-dimensional."[20]

---

20. Dan Millman, *Way of the Peaceful Warrior* (Tiburon, CA: H. J. Kramer, 1980), 26.

Goethe once said that "doubt grows with knowledge."[21] Doubt isn't something you want to deal with when faced with a threat. Knowing eliminates doubt. Knowing is a process of active awareness of the world around you. Knowing links knowledge with awareness, giving you a clear picture of your situation.

Robert Heinlein invented the word *grok* in his book *Stranger in a Strange Land*, which describes this process of knowing very well. To grok is to come to a complete and full understanding and awareness of a thing in real time. Or, as Heinlein described it: " . . . to understand so thoroughly that the observer becomes part of the observed . . . "[22] This is precisely what I mean when I use the word *knowing*. To Know is to place yourself in the moment and experience it fully. This experiencing brings understanding. This understanding shows you how you must act.

Knowing is not "immobilizing" a thing, isolating the thing from its environment. Knowing is a process that recognizes that everything is interconnected. Quantum physics has taught us not only that everything is interconnected, but also that imposing your will on what is observed changes it. Knowing is a process of perceiving without this immobilization. Bruce Lee once wrote that "awareness is without choice, without demand, without anxiety; in that state of mind, there is perception. Perception alone will resolve all our problems."[23] It is this characteristic that links this principle with one of the other five of our Magickal Artillery: To Keep Silent (which I will discuss in a moment).

---

21. Anthony Lejeune, ed., *The Concise Dictionary of Foreign Quotations* (London: Stacey International, 1998), 153.

22. Robert A. Heinlein, *Stranger in a Strange Land* (New York: Ace Books, 1987), 271.

23. Bruce Lee, *Tao of Jeet Kune Do*, 16.

This principle of knowing is the basis of the push-pull and hubud techniques in martial arts that I mentioned earlier. Knowing allows you to be in the moment, sense the energy around you, feel how it is flowing, and use that flow to your advantage. You detect the line that the force is taking and use that force against the person who sent it at you. Knowing allows you to make your opponents defeat themselves.

Knowing allows you to see through deception and illusion to grasp the true nature of your situation. Perception is a tricky business: things aren't always the way that they seem on the surface. Knowing allows you to dive below the surface and grasp a true and complete understanding of threats around you. Only then can you act appropriately and effectively. Knowing allows you to perceive the nature of your opponent's attack, which will give you the means to redirect it.

As I said in my book *Full Contact Magick*: the only way to control something is to understand it. The more you know about something, the more control you have over it. Knowledge is power. Magick is knowing. There is an old Japanese saying: "From one thing know ten thousand things." Knowing is the foundation from which accurate perception stems. From this foundation you can separate what is real from what is illusion. I'll return to this and show you some exercises to develop knowing, but first I need to speak to another principle that is linked to knowing: To Keep Silent.

To Keep Silent

As I mentioned a moment ago, another key principle of Magickal Artillery is "To Keep Silent." To Keep Silent is the process of scanning your environment to identify any threats that need to be dealt with. I summed up this axiom as one of my Warrior precepts in *Full Contact Magick*: *Perceive that which cannot be seen with the eye.* One cultivates this perception, this awareness, in silence.

You can't achieve knowing unless you've mastered the ability to Keep Silent.

To Keep Silent is the Japanese concept of "no mind" that allows you to be aware of everything around you while not being distracted by any particular thing. Dan Millman wrote that "silence is the warrior's art and meditation is his sword."[24] In order to perceive accurately, you need to become still within and without, clearing your mind of distractions. Once you have achieved this stillness, you can detect the subtle currents around you. Once you become still, you can access your instincts and emotions. This stillness will allow you to detect the emotions of your assailant. To Keep Silent is to become pure awareness.

Keeping silent is one of the principles of Magickal Artillery (the other being To Imagine) that is concerned with the process of drawing in energy. As I said, letting yourself become still and silent allows you to sense the energy currents around you. This not only allows you to select which energetic currents you will allow into your personal space, it also allows you to select which currents you want to deflect or ground out. It allows you to separate the energy you want to flow *through* you from the energy you want to flow *around* you.

Normally, our conscious perception is about 70 percent vision, with the remaining 30 percent divided between the four senses of hearing, smell, touch, and taste. To Keep Silent is the process of enhancing our perception, especially of our senses other than sight, in order to better perceive possible threats surrounding us. The practice of meditation allows us to enter what psychologists call *flow states* and what in yoga is called *Satori*. These are states of mind in which all of our senses are amplified and intensified. In order to defend yourself you need

---

24. Dan Millman, *Way of the Peaceful Warrior*, 82.

all five of your senses at maximum perceptive levels. Someone once asked me how one acquires this ability, "short of spending a couple of decades on a police force like you did." I have to say that it wasn't my police experience or training that gave me this ability. In fact, I know many police officers who spent as much or more time as I did on the mean streets who clearly never developed the abilities of knowing or of keeping silent. Not at all. What gave me this ability was the practice of meditation, specifically its use within disciplines such as the martial arts.

The discipline of meditation allows you to develop these flow states to make your defense more effective and efficient. There is an old saying in Karate: "Mind like water, mind like the moon." You want your mind to be like a still pond. This allows you to be aware of the slightest ripple in your awareness. A still mind accurately reflects the reality around it. Bruce Lee told us that "to understand the actual requires awareness, an alert and totally free mind."[25] Pure awareness is found in a mind free of thought. Satori is a true Warrior state of mind. Your whole life becomes awareness.

I must caution the reader that cultivating the ability to quickly identify the psychic attack does not necessarily mean that this should lead to instant retaliation. The principle "To Keep Silent" teaches us to wait patiently. Waiting patiently, sensing the flows emanating from your opponent, allows you to detect and defeat the attack. A weaker opponent, unable to stand the strain of waiting, often tries to deal the first blow. In that instant they reveal their strategy to you, allowing you to respond with a blow that is a combination of parry and attack, calculated to neutralize the strategy revealed by your less patient opponent. This is something the ancient Samurai understood well. To stand face to face with an enemy armed

---

25. Bruce Lee, *Tao of Jeet Kune Do*, 20.

with four feet of razor-sharp steel in this fashion required endless patience and awesome concentration.

To stand silent in the face of taunting, insults, and distractions isn't easy. I speak from experience. Yet you can do it. You *must* do it in a hostile situation. Remaining calm in such situations gives you a distinct advantage. Don't focus on the assailant's abusive and derogatory behavior. Focus on his body language. Get a feel for your opponent's energy. Become aware of what they are doing, not what they are saying. In a fight this allows you to respond quicker and use less force to control your assailant should they become violent. Often it permits you to deal with the situation without having resorted to physical means at all. It is this concentration, this intensity, this patience that I want you to achieve.

The same thing is true of psychic attacks. By shutting out the irrelevant things you can focus on the nature and flow of the negative energy. As soon as you sense the psychic attack, you become "silent" and examine it. You determine the true nature and extent of the attack. This allows you to respond to it effectively. You want to get this right the first time so that this doesn't turn into a lengthy process of strike and counterstrike.

The best way for the beginner to start to develop this ability is through meditation exercises. Meditation is a process of altering your mental state. Nothing special is required. All you need to practice meditation is the will to follow through with practice.

I want to caution you at this point. I'm talking about flow states here, not trance states. I'm talking about enhanced states of awareness, not simply altered states of awareness. Altered states, such as those brought on by medications, alcohol, and street drugs, do *not* enhance your defensive ability. In fact, they impair your perception. Drugs leave you with no control over the altered state that you find yourself in. Even worse, they can lead to debilitating and destructive addictions and brain damage, all of which further erodes your ability to defend yourself. As I pointed out earlier, drug addiction can lead to paranoia and false perceptions of attack.

Yes, some tribal cultures traditionally used drugs to achieve altered states of mind. While this is certainly true, it is also true that these cultures put those who used such mind-altering substances through rigorous training disciplines to give the user some control over the altered mental states achieved. They recognized that even a small error in judgment could bring about disastrous consequences, even to an experienced person. Part of the reason that many of these ancients used drugs to achieve altered states was that they didn't know any other way to achieve altered states of consciousness. We can no longer use that excuse. Street drugs and chemical hallucinogens destroy your brain cells. They don't clear your mind, they cloud it. They don't improve your perception, they dull it. Worse, the symptoms of some street drugs include paranoia, which will give the user the false impression that they are under psychic or physical attack.

Drugs are risky, limiting, and unnecessary. They won't help you to face your fears; they will cause your fears to overwhelm you. They impair your ability to face the challenges of life. They are simply a form of escape. Drugs and/or alcohol may mask the symptoms of a psychic attack for a while, but they leave you even more vulnerable to attack. You don't need drugs or alcohol to face your fears. Courage is fear holding on a minute longer, as General George Patton put it.[26]

---

26. Gen. George Patton, "Quote DB," http://www.quotedb.com/quotes/4120 (accessed 27 September 2007).

You can't defend yourself, psychically or otherwise, if you aren't prepared to face your assailant. You must become the master of your situation. You need to remove the difficulties and challenges in your life by overcoming them, not covering them up.

Let me repeat the warning that I voiced at the beginning of this book: If you are using street drugs such as crack cocaine or crystal methamphetamine, you *will* develop paranoia. Always. You will very likely think that you are experiencing psychic attacks. *It isn't a psychic attack you are experiencing; it is the symptoms of the damage that you are doing to your brain.* You need to immediately seek professional medical help and enter drug rehabilitation. I hope that if you are in this situation, you'll still have enough insight reading this to seek help. If not, I hope you've got some loyal friends or family who will intervene to save you. Otherwise your life is likely to be short and unpleasant.

Meditation

The best way to develop knowing and awareness is to practice meditation. If you've never attempted meditation before, you'll probably find that it is best to start in a place that is relatively quiet and where you aren't likely to be disturbed. People in North America usually find that it's best to start practicing meditation in a comfortable seated posture. I would rather that you learned to meditate in a standing posture from the ancient Chinese art of Chi Kung called "Entering Tranquility," which you can use to enter flow states. Chi Kung is a practice involving the movement of life energy, or chi, in the body. You'll recognize this posture from my book *Full Contact Magick.*

Ultimately, I want you to learn to work from the Entering Tranquility posture because if you are on your feet when the psychic attack comes in, you can quickly fall into this posture and defend yourself. I used to meditate in this posture in the middle of a busy workout room at the police station. Like me, you'll learn through practice to shut out the activity around you at will. Later in this book, I'll give you some examples to illustrate this.

The Entering Tranquility posture works like this: Stand with your feet about shoulder width apart, toes pointing forward. Shift your weight slightly forward onto the balls of your feet. Do not lock your knees. By this I do not mean having your knees so loose that you collapse in a heap—just don't make them rigid. Keep your knees spread apart slightly, as if you were sitting on a horse. Don't allow your knees to flex inward. It helps to imagine that you have something like a basketball held between your knees keeping them apart. Keep your abdomen relaxed and "soft."

Breathe naturally into your lower lungs, letting your abdomen naturally expand and contract. Don't breathe by flexing your chest. Use your diaphragm instead. Have you ever noticed how an infant breathes when she is on her back? Her stomach rises and falls as she breathes. In Western society we learn to breathe with our chests as we mature. I don't want you to breathe with your chest here. I want you to breathe down into your abdomen.

Now imagine that someone has attached a string to the top of your head and is pulling upward. This will straighten your back and roll your backside under your spine to support it better. Let your arms hang at your sides with your palms turned to face behind you. Lightly touch the tip of your tongue to the roof of your mouth.

Relax. Do not allow any part of your body to tense up. If your body is tight or tense, this will restrict the flow of chi or energy and eventually cause distracting discomfort. In this posture, all of the energy channels should be free. Breathe naturally and deeply. Don't rely on shallow chest breathing. Relax your abdomen and let the diaphragm drop, drawing air deep into the lungs. Focus on your breathing at first. Take a deep breath in, hold it a moment, inhale a little more, and then exhale completely. Once you have exhaled, hold a moment, and then exhale a little more before taking the next breath. After a while you will do this without thinking about it. Inhaling a little extra before exhaling and vice versa helps you to do this deep breathing with less discomfort. If you are distracted or preoccupied, imagine that your concerns are being expelled from you each time that you exhale.

It is common to experience tingling or sensations of heat or cold in your arms when the chi is flowing. When you are doing magick, you should feel this energy flow. If you don't, check to see what it is that is blocking the energy flow and correct it.

If you get dizzy while trying to find the right rhythm for your breathing, you are hyperventilating. Slow your breathing rate down and this dizziness will disappear. Yawning isn't necessarily an indication that you are relaxing; it may be an indication that you are holding your breath too long on the inhale part of the cycle. Coughing can be an indication that you are holding too long on the exhale part of the cycle.

As you exhale, imagine "dark air" or negative energy leaving your body. As you inhale, imagine "light air," "pure air," or positive energy entering your body. Continue until you are filled with pure energy and the dark energy is no longer flowing out of you.

Whether you are standing or sitting, an upright posture is extremely important in meditation. It improves breathing and the flow of energy or chi. Sitting slumped over decreases the flow of oxygen. Eventually it will lead to distracting discomfort. If you are seated, you can use the same trick that we used in Entering Tranquility to achieve this: imagine that a string is attached to the top of your head and is pulling you up.

Now that you've established a proper posture for meditation, you will need something to practice focusing your attention on. Since our natural perception is predominantly visual, we'll use visual exercises to start with. Later you should experiment with exercises involving the other senses: sound, smell, taste, and touch. To begin with, I strongly suggest using a visual object that moves. Movement captures our attention: advertisers often use action and motion in television commercials to capture our interest. Typical examples are:

- A candle flame
- The second hand of a watch
- A feather suspended from the ceiling on a string

Relax. The latest studies indicate that suppression of the twelve to twenty-four cycles-per-second beta waves in your brain allows your inner vision to unfold. What this means is that you are shutting down the left side of your brain to allow the right side to work more freely. It is hard to achieve a calm state of awareness if the brain is rushing along at twenty-four cycles per second.

Give yourself to the moment. Become the moment. Put expectations out of your mind in these exercises. Accept what comes. You're learning to cultivate awareness here. Absorb every aspect of the thing that you are focusing on. Simply experience the object in front of you. Don't think about it. You want the impressions that come to you to originate in the intuitive part of you, where they will arrive without conscious thought. Beginners often find that their undisciplined minds tend to wander. Don't try to force this process. Don't mentally kick yourself in the butt if you catch yourself going off on some train of thought or other. Just say to yourself "thinking," and start again. You want to shut down the incessant internal dialogue that many people constantly have within themselves.

With practice, you will be able to focus on the object for longer and longer periods without thinking. The goal here is to try to hold the object as long as possible without outside thoughts intruding. Eventually this will improve your concentration. The longer you can maintain an image in your mind, the greater the magickal effect.

How much you meditate each day depends on your needs and your level of competence. It is a good practice to gradually work up from ten minutes a day to thirty minutes a day. Don't rush things. It usually takes up to a year to master basic meditation.

Once you have achieved some success with this meditation technique, try looking at the shadows of things rather than at the objects themselves. For example, when viewing a tree in sunlight, most people look at the pattern of light as reflected by the leaves. Instead, try meditating on the patterns made by the shadows. This technique will train your mind to look at things more completely. It will teach you to look for the unexpected. Using shadows cast by natural sunlight is the best place to start; such shadows naturally move, which tends to hold the beginner's attention.

Try doing this meditation with no particular focus. Simply become aware of exactly what is happening around you. Use all of your senses. Close your eyes and listen to what is happening around you. Choose a sound and focus on it. If you have a small pond with a waterfall in your backyard, you can focus on the sound of the waterfall. Try to hold that sound in your mind to the exclusion of all others. You will probably surprise yourself with the number of sounds around you that you weren't aware of before.

Try closing your eyes and simply becoming aware of what is happening in your own body. Awareness of what your body is doing will often give you warning of impending attacks. This awareness is what is meant by the words *intuition* and *instincts*. Cultivate your self-awareness.

There is a scene in the movie *The Last Samurai* in which Captain Algren is repeatedly being knocked to the ground by the senior Samurai instructor he is practicing with. The son of the Samurai leader runs up to Algren, who has once again been dumped on the ground by his instructor. The Samurai leader's son tells Algren: "Too many mind! Mind of school. Mind of people watching. Mind of enemy. No mind!" He is referring to the principle of "no mind" that I mentioned earlier in this chapter. Algren is distracted by thoughts of all of the things around him in the training area. His mind is not like a still pond that reflects the reality surrounding it. Later in the movie, when Algren finally grasps the concept of no mind, he finds that he is finally able to match the ability of his instructor.

The Warrior must find this place of no mind. Author David Gemmell calls it "the illusion of elsewhere."[27] I mentioned that I used to practice meditation in the police gym while standing in Entering Tranquility. This allowed me to practice shutting out distractions while in that "illusion of elsewhere." Two sides of the gym were windows giving a panoramic view of downtown Vancouver. I would choose some element from this panorama to focus on. Alternately, I would choose some sound or smell in the training area to focus on. I would practice being aware of things around me without thinking about them. I would become aware of people moving toward or away from

---

27. David Gemmell, *White Wolf* (London: Corgi Books, 2003), 223.

me. I learned to anticipate their movements. You can practice this in the office lunchroom, in the office, in a park, or at a family gathering. The possibilities are endless. A variation that I'm fond of involves going out in a field on a windy day to do my meditation. I close my eyes and sense the flow of the wind. I try to sense when and where the next gust is going to come from. If you try this, before long you'll find that you can turn to face the wind before the wind starts up.

If you have not meditated before, or have not done so for a long time, you will often experience a rush of unbidden thoughts, images, and sensations. This isn't a psychic attack. These are hypnogogic images, caused by the release of built-up stress inside of you. People with few outlets for accumulated stress tend to store up this psychic garbage in their mind. Meditation creates an outlet, letting all of this stressful energy come rushing out suddenly. This can take the form of racing thoughts. Sometimes it takes the form of impressions of something or someone at the edge of your range of vision: you turn your head to look and there is nothing there. It can come on as unusual or unpleasant feelings—an odd smell, or a voice. Sometimes the release of this tension produces a headache. This is normal. Let it pass and start again. As the store of built-up energy diminishes, these hypnogogic images will diminish and disappear.

If these images overwhelm you, there's a simple technique you can use to dispel them quickly, utilizing one of the mantras that I discuss elsewhere in this book. First, focus on the images and sensations that are making you uneasy. Imagine that they are a dark cloud within you. Then, shout out loud (or in your mind) the word "Haa!" three times: "Haa! Haa! Haa!" With each shout imagine the cloud (and the sensations within it) being expelled from you. Imagine this dark cloud receding into the distance until it vanishes from sight.

So, what does this give you? Remember I told you that many cops never developed this ability simply by being cops? Imagine one of those cops encounters a man on the street, looks at him, and may (if the cop is lucky) have a vague awareness that something is wrong. Very likely this is verbalized by the phrase "He doesn't look/feel right." Asked to describe exactly what is meant by that, you find the cop at a loss for words.

When I encounter this same man, I use my total awareness: Knowing. I see his trembling hands clenching into fists, the tensing posture that indicates he is setting himself up for a strike. I see the flaring nostrils and hear his rapid breathing. I detect the panic in the sound of his unnecessarily loud voice. I smell his sweat and know that he has been using alcohol and drugs. I see his dilated pupils, his eyes swiveling onto the part of my body that he is considering punching. Most importantly, I feel that strike coming before it starts. I don't just look at him; I know him, I experience him, I read his entire body like a book, I feel the flow of his energy. Intuitively, I feel that he is about to attack, which gives me the ability to prevent the attack.

Now let's use the example of a psychic attack, which is much more subtle. The untrained person, if they notice anything at all, is going to feel a vague sense of unease. Eventually they will start to exhibit some or all of the symptoms that I listed in chapter 1. The person trained in these meditation techniques is going to sense the subtle beginnings of changes within their body as it reacts to this energy. This will instantly alert them to the flow and nature of the energy involved. Before they are consciously aware of this psychic attack, their mind will be starting to react in order to redirect the flow and shield themselves.

Once you develop your awareness you can identify and locate the threat. You can link this ability to your working with energy (which I will discuss in chapter 7). Working with energy gives you an awareness of the "feel" of energy. This familiarization becomes part of your enhanced awareness: it will allow you to effectively detect the flow of negative energy projected at you, the first step in developing an effective psychic defense. Yet before we get to detecting and using energy, I want to focus on another key element of psychic defense: your will.

Will

FOUR

Will

An eye like Mars, to threaten and command.

—Shakespeare, *Hamlet*

Will is fiercely focusing your intent on your desire. Will is the act of asserting your intention. Will directs the expected result or outcome of magick. It directs the attack for the assailant and the expected result or outcome of the defense for the defender. This could include anything that the human mind can conceive, from financial loss to death. The more focused your will is, the better the results you will obtain. To be most effective, the attack should be focused on the victim's point of vulnerability. Focusing on the attacker's vulnerabilities is equally important to the defender. Expanding your awareness helps you to identify these vulnerabilities.

Another reason for expanding your awareness, as I asked you to do in the previous chapter, is related to will. Enhanced awareness can give you the "early warning" you need to be most effective and help you to identify your opponent's vulnerabilities and take advantage of them. Through arrogance or lackadaisical attitude, assailants don't always set up their own defense, assuming that the victim will not or cannot respond to their attack. People who believe that no one would dare oppose them or that no one is as powerful as they are can be made to learn the hard way that they are in error. This arrogance is a major weakness in an opponent, which should be exploited in your defense. Improving your awareness allows you to exploit such weaknesses.

In any psychic battle, the person with the greater will usually emerges victorious. Thus, will and discipline are essential elements of your defense. It is discipline that allows you to maintain control of the disparate forces that surround you and contact you. Will or intent is what allows you to direct your energy to the right place and seal the cracks in your defenses. Without will, the magickal energy that you release will be diffuse and ineffective.

Experimentation has proved that your will affects your universe. Over the last forty years multiple experiments have been conducted utilizing people trained in meditation. These experiments utilize random number generators: these computerized devices randomly generate sequences of ones and zeros. In every case, when groups of people simply meditate in the presence of such devices (without focusing their will on these devices), the devices become less random. The stream of numbers generated by the device becomes more coherent.

In 1995, Dr. Dean Radin and his colleagues conducted experiments in which random generators were set up in five different cities while the verdict of the O. J. Simpson murder trial was being announced.[28] Here you had millions of people focusing their attention briefly on this one event. *All five random number generators created more coherent, less random streams of numbers during the instant that the verdict was announced.* The odds against this occurring by chance are 50,000 to 1.

Dr. Jeffry Palmer puts it this way: "Knowing the value of positive thought energy allows us to become sensitive to negative energy."[29] Palmer reports that "in 1993 a study encouraged by one of the world's leading physicists was undertaken in Washington, D. C. to determine if focused meditation could have an effect on that city's crime rate. The results were astonishing. During the weeks that several volunteers meditated, crime rates fell dramatically by 25 percent! This was no accident. This was scientifically validated and proven to be an effective means of countering the criminal inclinations of a very large group of people . . . an entire city in fact."[30] I told you earlier how we can all be affected by the negative energy absorbed into the objects in our world. You are equally affected by positive energy in your vicinity. Imagine what we could do if enough of us were putting positive energy into the universe. Clearly your will has an effect on your world. All you have to do is learn to use it effectively.

There is an old Zen adage, "munen muso," which means "where there is no intention, there is no thought of moving." "The reason why motivation assists in producing larger effects in the lab—and probably in life—is because of the psychologi-

---

28. Dean Radin, PhD, in *What the Bleep!?: Down the Rabbit Hole* (DVD, 2006).

29. Jeffry R. Palmer, PhD, "The Nature of Thought Energy," Project Sanctuary, http://projectsanctuary.com/main/modules.php?name=News&file=article&sid=58 (accessed 12 November 2005).

30. Ibid.

cal component," Dr. Dean Radin tells us. "When we are highly motivated to perceive information, to perceive something, to do something, to wish something . . . we have much more that we bring to bear, in terms of our attention and intention, toward that goal. I think the name of the game, at least from the mind side of this equation, is *attention*. The more attention that can be brought to bear for a longer period of time on a goal, the larger or more precise, more achievable the result. That's why motivation is important. Motivation is a natural way of focusing attention."[31] This is exactly what will is: focusing your attention on a chosen objective. For years magicians have realized that a strong will is the key to magickal success, and these experiments show how that works.

In Eastern philosophies, magickal energy is known as *chi*. There is an old Karate adage: "Chi follows I," which could be restated as "energy follows intent." Note the similarity between this and my Wiccan definition of magick: "Causing change by directing energy with one's will." In Japanese martial arts the perfect striking technique is 80 to 90 percent chi. This chi is directed to the target by the will or intent (I) of the martial artist. Your punch is therefore not a bony hammer, but a connecting bridge channeling the chi from you to the opponent. Ideally, only a small portion of the technique is physical strength. Obviously, in combat this energy is accessed instantaneously. It wouldn't be of any use to the martial artist if it could not be accessed instantaneously.

Another way of stating this is to say that chi (energy) follows your intent or will. Will is the steering mechanism that directs the energy to the objective. Without will, the energy

---

31. Dean Radin, PhD, "Interview with Dean Radin, Part I," http://www .whatthebleep.com/herald12/radin5.shtml (accessed 18 October 2007).

that you sent out wouldn't go anywhere. It would simply disperse randomly into the universe.

To Will is another of those principles that form part of my concept of Magickal Artillery. To Will is to pull the trigger and let your magick fly. Will is unwavering purpose. Will is channeling your awareness, focusing intensely and precisely on your objective. Will is clearly defining your objective. If you don't do this, then your magick isn't going to go where you want it to go. Will and concentration go hand in hand.

In martial arts, you want to concentrate your force into as small an area as possible. This is the principle that makes a punch so effective in Karate: energy (chi) is concentrated and focused with intent. The same principle applies in magick. If you simply broadcast the energy that you raise in no particular direction, or with a very vague or general focus, it will not have much effect. But if all of your energy is focused on a very narrow purpose or on a very clearly defined goal, it will invariably succeed.

Interestingly enough, people who are adept at out-of-body experiences (OBEs) don't usually seem to be troubled by psychic attacks. Why? They've had to develop their will to achieve OBEs. This ability serves them well when it comes to protecting themselves from outside influences.

To Dare

If you do not trust in your magickal power, its strength and energy will be weakened. Belief gives your magick a firm foundation and makes your magick more effective. Belief in your abilities grants genuine power. In psychic self-defense the force of will is paramount, and belief reinforces this. To Dare is another principle of Magickal Artillery.

Some of you with military backgrounds will recognize "To Dare" in the motto of the British Special Air Service Regiment

(SAS): "Who Dares Wins." To defend yourself you must have faith in yourself and in your abilities. To Dare is to let go of your inhibitions and doubts and face your fears. Magick, and especially magickal defenses, simply will not work for you if you don't believe that they will.

I've frequently seen children succeed in magick where adults fail. This is because no one has yet tried to teach them that what they are attempting is supposed to be impossible. Learning to dare means recapturing this childlike audacity. We see this in the Tarot card The Fool, on which the Fool is about to risk a jump into the abyss. That is using the "illusion of elsewhere" I mentioned earlier. You empty your mind of fear and fight from a place of "no mind."

You can't protect yourself through what might be called purity of spirit. "Calling down the white light" isn't enough to defend you from psychic attack. While you're sitting in the white light the enemy is out there in the darkness waiting for an opportunity. Focusing on purity and light may make you feel good, but it doesn't alter the emotions or intent of your assailant unless you project it outward, toward your assailant.

Meditating upon abstract principles such as peace, harmony, protection, and love does make it harder for negative influences to entrain or connect with your subconscious mind. That is probably where the idea that purity protecting you comes from. This technique certainly helps protect you, but it doesn't remove the cause of the threat. This "sitting in the white light" approach doesn't address the nature of the problem. Instead, it's like the child who hides under their bed covers: an action that might make them feel more secure for a time, but they're only hiding from the problem.

Prayer isn't that effective either. Prayer can be helpful to aid your focus and bolster your spirit, and even to whip up emotion to raise the needed energy for your defense. But if all you're doing is sitting on your ass asking some entity out there to do it all for you, then you're going to be in for a big disappointment. Invocation of external potencies should not be viewed as asking an outside entity to help you. Rather, think of it as attuning yourself to protective energy. I don't worship; I entrain, I connect, I immerse myself in divinity. The divine is inseparable from the everyday world. This is related to the principle of entrainment that I will describe in a later chapter.

By all means, choose a protective God-form that attracts you. Set up an altar with objects that honor this God-form, and regularly acknowledge them in meditations and prayers. Wear a piece of jewelry dedicated to them. These actions are simply focusing tools to help you imagine yourself surrounded by protective energy, allowing you to achieve the correct resonance. I'll describe focusing tools, as well as specific techniques to surround yourself with such energy, later in this book.

Staying in a mystical state that aligns you with certain vibrations only lasts as long as you remain in that state. Once you drop your guard or get distracted, the attack simply begins anew. Negative energy directed at you will affect the people around you if it can't connect with you. The disharmony that this creates around you will disrupt your concentration and pull you out of your mystical state, exposing you to the attack.

I'm not saying that striving for purity is a useless occupation. You certainly won't be doing yourself a favor if you bring yourself down to the level of your assailant. Purity does help you align yourself to keep out negative vibrations. It may enhance your belief and confidence, which, in turn, enhances your ability to withstand attacks. It provides fewer "chinks" for an attack to get in. Similarly, the old adage that "they can't attack you if you don't believe they can" has some merit. Fear of the power of the assailant can enhance the assailant's assault. However, you'll need to take a more active and assertive approach if you want to protect yourself effectively.

Will and Quantum Mechanics

Let's set the concept of will aside for a moment and take a quick look at some basics of quantum mechanics and how they relate to our reality and our magick. In the physical world, you perceive this book you're holding and the chair you're sitting on as "solid." You don't perceive the book and the chair as a network of atoms flickering in and out of reality, nor do you perceive that both the book and the chair actually consist mostly of vast empty spaces between the atoms that make them up. You don't perceive that these atoms are made up of miniscule particles that behave more like waves than particles, and which pop in and out of a vast field of infinite potentiality.

The Planck scale is the basement level of reality, the smallest that we can get: the Planck length is a millimeter divided by a hundred thousand billion billion billion.[32] The British physicist Sir Roger Penrose has demonstrated that reality as we know it is created out of the quantum information encoded on a "unified field" at the Planck scale, which is the substrate of all life. It is at this level that the information and potentiality that creates the entire universe is stored. Penrose shows us that the phenomenon we call consciousness may ultimately be a Planck scale phenomenon. Consciousness comes from the Planck scale field where all potential reality is stored. Magick is reaching into the possibilities in this sea of consciousness at the Planck level with your consciousness, your will, to make things manifest.

---

32.   Precisely 0.00000000000000000000000000000001616 mm

One of the principles that explains how these quantum particles pop out of this field of potentiality to create what we experience as reality is Erwin Schrödinger's wave equation, also known as the *wave function*. The Schrödinger wave equation tells us that reality is the outcome of interactions of waves of probabilities. When observed, these waves manifest as what we have been taught to call matter and energy. These probability waves overlap and continue infinitely, binding the entire universe together into an unbroken whole. The universe is a matrix of interconnected waves of potentiality. Everything is connected to and affects everything else, just as some of our ancient myths tell us.

Schrödinger's equation predicts the rate at which a wave function changes with time. It tells us that the only thing we can predict is the wave function; it predicts the probability that the measurable attributes of a particle will have a certain value. Schrödinger's uncertainty principle can allow us to predict either the position or the velocity of a particle, but not both. I'll come back to this in chapter 6 when I describe the classical dual slit interference experiment.

Only being able to predict the wave function has some interesting implications. Schrödinger's equation allows one to compute the probability that a molecule of water will escape through the walls of a sealed glass jar and be found outside of it. Because all matter has the properties of quantum duality, Schrödinger's uncertainty principle demonstrates that there is a calculable possibility that if you took a trip somewhere, leaving your cat at home, that you might bump into your cat at your destination. Until the event happens (in other words, until the observation is made), only the probabilities exist. At the instant that the observation (or measurement) is made, the values of the attribute become certain and Schrödinger's equation with its probabilities is said to "collapse" to an actual event with a probability equal to 1. The information or potentiality of the unified field at the Planck level of existence helps decide what form the potentialities will become when they collapse into our reality. Magick is using our will, our intent, to influence the way that this potentiality collapses into reality.

According to physicist David Bohm, quantum particles can be understood simply as projections of a higher-dimensional reality. As I noted, information within the quantum wave determines the outcome: this information is potentially active everywhere but only becomes active when and where it enters into the energy of an observed particle. Another way of looking at this is to say that all systems exist simultaneously in all quantum mechanically possible states until an observer interacts to "collapse" the "state vector" and obtain an observation. A quantum state vector fully specifies any quantum mechanical state in which a quantum mechanical system can be. It is the act of observation, the will of the observer, that causes the "state vector" to "collapse" into reality. In other words, you create your own reality.

Of course, you are doing this constantly, to one extent or another, without being aware of it. The degree of influence you have upon the process may be negligible most of the time. Many of the variables involved are so strong that whatever influence you direct upon the process may not make much difference at all. Yet you can exert your influence. If you do, it will have a measurable effect.

I encourage you to explore the subjects of quantum physics, psychokinesis, and "intentionality" in more detail by reading astronaut Edgar Mitchell's 1996 book, *The Way of the Explorer*. The implication for magick within this view of intentionality is this: one could say that practicing magick is the process of causing the variables of Schrödinger's wave equation or "state vector" to collapse in the place required to achieve the desired result. So magick is exerting your will upon the available waves of probabilities in order to choose the reality you want and to cause the variables to collapse that wave into the desired reality.

The key to this process is will. Will is the intent that causes the probabilities to collapse into your desired reality. I will describe how to use your imagination in conjunction with your will to accomplish this later in this book. Suffice it to say that maintaining your focus is essential in magick. Will helps you avoid diversions and eliminate that which distracts you from your defense. Will helps you focus on your objective. Will allows you to focus your energy, making your defensive magick more effective. It is focusing your will that causes the waves of probabilities to coalesce into the reality that you desire.

Discipline and Decisiveness

As I mentioned at the beginning of this chapter, will is inextricably linked to strong self-discipline. Self-discipline is essential in psychic self-defense. Discipline trains the mind, which is one of the Lesser Magickal Weapons that I listed in *Full Contact Magick*. Self-discipline and persistence will allow you to overcome any psychic attack.

Negativity and depression can hamper your psychic defenses. Negativity helps the negative get in, and unhappiness and depression can be gateways for the negative energy of others. Modern society daily places us in many situations that breed such unhappiness. Alleviating depression can help to protect you from psychic attacks. The lessons contained in difficult life situations are often unpleasant, but just as often life will not change for the better unless we take such lessons to heart. Will and self-discipline can help you to overcome difficult situations.

Quick and decisive action is often required for any form of self-defense. When you are under attack, you often don't have much time to decide what course of action to take. But that does not mean that you should rush into a situation. Careful consideration and planning are often the keys to success. However, it is also true that one doesn't always have a lot of time to respond.

General Patton once said that "A good plan, violently executed now, is better than a perfect plan executed next week."[33] In psychic self-defense, what is often more important is not which decision you make but rather that you take decisive action quickly. I have found over and over again in my police and magickal work that there is usually more than one way to accomplish something. Make a decision and move ahead. General Sun Tzu once said that "the quality of a decision is like the well-timed swoop of a falcon which enables it to strike and destroy its victim."[34] Timely action can often save the day.

Hoping that the nasty stuff will all go away isn't the answer. Doing nothing isn't going to help your situation. You must overcome the threat to move forward and continue developing. If you don't, then this attack becomes a "guardian of the threshold" that will obstruct you on many levels.

Similar to muscles, the will responds and grows with regular exercise. Exercising both the mind and the body requires self-discipline, a very effective tool in warding off psychic attacks. A sensitive assailant can easily detect a lazy, undisciplined mind. Such a mind is less likely to defend itself, because it cannot control itself. Conversely, a sensitive assailant is less likely to attempt

---

33. Gen. George Patton, "General George S. Patton, Jr. Quotations," http://www.generalpatton.com/quotes.html (accessed 26 September 2007).

34. Sun Tzu (trans. by Thomas Cleary), *The Art of War*, 1991, 35.

a psychic attack if what they detect is a disciplined mind with a strong will. Disciplined people are difficult targets.

Magickal Weapons

Many of the books on psychic self-defense that I've read suggest protecting yourself with crystals, objects, or Magickal Weapons of some sort. It's true that these weapons can be helpful focusing tools. But I am reminded of what Henry David Thoreau said in *Walden*: "But lo! Men have become the tools of their tools."

I suppose one cannot think of defense without thinking of weapons. Weapons have certainly appeared in many ancient works of magick. Gardner borrowed the idea of Magickal Weapons from ceremonial magick when he laid down the basic structure of Wiccan ritual practice. Gardner mentions the sword and the athame among the "working tools" presented to the initiate.[35] In ceremonial magick they are often referred to as "Elemental Weapons."[36] In *The Greater Key of Solomon* the Magician is cautioned: "In order to properly carry out the greatest and most important Operations of the Art, various Instruments are necessary . . . "[37] *The Greater Key of Solomon* instructs the magician to "beat or strike the air"[38] with his sword while making his conjurations and prayers. When most people think of psychic self-defense, they think of the use of weapons to protect themselves.

Magickal Weapons are part of a Judeo-Christian magickal system that treats energy as an external process. These same

---

35. Janet Farrar and Stewart Farrar, *A Witches' Bible, Volume II: The Rituals* (Custer, WA: Phoenix Publishing, 1984), 19.

36. Dion Fortune, *Moon Magic* (York Beach, ME: Samuel Weiser, 1978), 80.

37. *The Greater Key of Solomon*, book two, chapter VIII, introductory paragraph.

38. Ibid., book one, chapter III.

systems hold that the magick Circle is primarily a means of defense against dangerous forces of nature and psychic attacks. My psychic defense doesn't rely on fixed defensive positions and external forces. General Patton once said: "Fixed fortifications are monuments to man's stupidity."[39] I don't place my reliance on Magickal Weapons. The magick that I'm teaching you is an internal process. Everything that you need to defend yourself from psychic attack is in you right now.

Many of the ancient techniques of psychic attack involve substitution or sympathetic magick—for example, making a "voodoo" doll and acting upon this as if it were your victim. Another more gruesome example is substituting an animal for the victim and working on the animal. All these substitutes are focusing tools for the magician's will. You don't need such substitutes to do magick. You don't need "tools" like this to focus your will. You can do very well without them. I do all the time.

I pointed out in my book *Full Contact Magick* that carrying a weapon does not make you a Warrior. Weapons are simply an extension of ourselves. Your assailant's choice of weapons tells you much about your assailant. Your choice of weapons to defend or attack reveals much about you to your opponent. You must master the use of these weapons or they will master you.

I refer to the tools found in the typical Pagan ritual as Magickal Weapons. As I noted in *Full Contact Magick*, Wiccans have adopted several sets of Magickal Weapons from Celtic mythology. I modified the four double groupings of Weapons that Steve Blamires listed in his book *Glamoury*[40] to create the five double groupings that I use in my practice. The fifth

---

39. Gen. George Patton, "General George S. Patton, Jr. Quotations," http://www.generalpatton.com/quotes.html (accessed 26 September 2007).

40. Steve Blamires, *Glamoury: Magic of the Celtic Green World* (St. Paul, MN: Llewellyn, 1995), 292.

grouping is something that Blamires did not include in his list: Spirit.

In my system, each group of Magickal Weapons is associated with an element. For Air (east): the dagger (athame) or sword. For Fire (south): the wand or spear. For Water (west): the chalice or cauldron. For Earth (north): the pentacle, shield, or stone. The Magickal Weapon of Spirit is your mind. (Note: I spell the word *Weapon* with a capital *W* in this work when I am using the word in reference to a Magickal Weapon.)

The Greater Magickal Weapons are Spirit, the sword, the spear, the cauldron, and the shield. The Lesser Magickal Weapons are your mind, the athame (dagger), the wand, the chalice, and the pentacle or stone. I classify Spirit as a Greater Magickal Weapon because it is the source of energy used in magickal work. Energy is useless until it is directed by intent. It is Spirit that gives you access to the other four elements and unifies them. I classify mind as a Lesser Magickal Weapon because it is your mind that gives you the ability to use the other four lesser weapons. A wooden pole can be a broom handle or a quarter-staff depending on how it is used.

As I pointed out in *Full Contact Magick*, you have to master yourself before you can master these Weapons. You have to start with the Greater Magickal Weapon of Spirit and the Lesser Magickal Weapon of mind. Intent comes from your mind. Your mind is the key to all of the Magickal Weapons, Greater and Lesser. "He that would govern others," Philip Massinger once wrote, "first should be the master of himself."[41] None of these Weapons is of any use unless you've trained your mind to use them. They are all extensions of your mind. Your mind can ultimately replace all of them.

---

41. Philip Massinger, *The Duke of Milan* (1623), Act 1, Scene ii.

Many Pagans surround themselves with ritual tools and paraphernalia such as these Magickal Weapons in order to provide a defense against negative forces. Their homes and ritual spaces are crammed full of all manner of props and ritual gear. I discussed the use of such ritual tools and weapons in my book *Wiccan Warrior*. Many people become so dependent on this ritual gear that they cannot practice magick without it.

On television and in martial arts movies, fights are exaggerated and go on endlessly. In real life, the best moves are simple, subtle, quick, and devastatingly effective. I urge you to apply this principle to psychic self-defense. You don't need to do complicated, lengthy rituals to do effective protective magick. You don't need a lot of Magickal Weapons and paraphernalia. As Bruce Lee once said, "Simplicity is the shortest distance between two points."[42]

Many of us are so used to doing magick in ritual Circles that we forget that we can do magick with no Circle at all—any time, in any place. When the martial artist in the middle of a fight decides to launch a punch or kick, they don't first go through an elaborate process of cleansing, setting up altars, circumambulating with the elements, calling the quarters, drawing down the deities, and so on. They instantaneously connect with the energy and send it out through their fist or foot. The whole process of energizing and focusing with the will takes a split second. Psychic self-defense is no different.

You don't need to do a ritual to protect yourself. You don't need to cast an elaborate ritual Circle and fill it with magickal props. I see so many people get lost in elaborate rituals as if it were simply this process alone that was creating the energy used in the magickal defence. You can do magick to protect yourself where you are right now without any Circle, without

---

42. Bruce Lee, *Tao of Jeet Kune Do*, 12.

any paraphernalia, without any ritual. All you have to do is raise energy and direct it. Marco Rodriguez, a fellow police officer and Ceremonial Magician, once put it this way: "If it was the tools that made magick, we'd be mechanics, not magicians."[43]

I'm not suggesting that you should abandon ritual altogether and sell off all of your ritual gear. Ritual can be a very effective tool and I encourage my students to master it. Many of the ritual implements used in magickal rituals can be used to focus and enhance the magickal working. All that I am saying is when push comes to shove, you only need one thing to raise and direct energy to protect yourself: you. You are the source of the magickal energy.

Beginners find ritual tools such as Magickal Weapons useful to help focus magickal energy. I know I did. Like the weapons that you practice with in the dojo, they can be used as extensions of yourself. Just remember that Magickal Weapons don't raise and direct the energy: you do. Magickal Weapons only work for you once you have developed the ability to raise energy and let it flow from you. Magickal Weapons can only be used to help you direct the energy.

Candles are a common magickal focusing tool. In a typical magickal ritual, candles of particular colors are selected, decorated, anointed, and set alight. Novices often get the idea in their heads from this that it is the candle that is generating the magick. This is not the case. You are. Neither is the candle directing the magickal energy to its source. Again, you are. The candle is simply a tool to help focus your intent. During the course of the ritual and later in the course of your day, your mind keeps coming back to the recollection that this candle is steadily burning on the altar. This repetitive recollection inten-

---

43.   E-mail to me from Officer Marco Rodriguez of the Los Angeles Police Department, dated 31 March 2000.

sifies your magick as it brings your defensive intent back into focus again and again. You are doing the protective magick. The candle is just a tool that you are using to help you do it.

Another simple example of a focusing tool is writing your intention on a piece of paper. Some people suggest that you place this paper over your heart chakra to assist you in meditating on your intent.[44] All that you really need to do is to put it in some prominent, significant, or unusual place. This will help bring it to your attention over and over again. One technique I've encountered involves putting the name of the person who is causing you problems on a piece of paper and then putting this piece of paper in your freezer. This isn't so much sympathetic magick as it is helping your mind focus on the idea that you are freezing up your assailant's ability to get at you.

If you are going to set up a defensive ritual space, ritual paraphernalia can help you define its parameters and purpose in your mind. Setting up ritual paraphernalia is an action that signals to your subconscious mind that something special is happening, as these actions are something out of the ordinary routine of our lives. Such an action signals to your mind as well as the world that you are accessing the Magician archetype. By surrounding yourself with ritual paraphernalia, you are encircling yourself with things that remind you what your purpose is in that ritual Circle. If you're a novice, this can be very helpful. If you're setting them up around a particular site or dwelling, then the memory of these objects being there brings your mind back into focus on the defensive purpose, over and over, just like in candle magick. It is this mental action that is the key to the objects' success. To be magickal, you must believe that you are magickal.

---

44. Joseph Rinoza Plazo, "Psychic 101, Psychic Self-Defense," http://www.psychic101.com/self-defense-psychic.html (accessed 22 October 2007).

Items of ritual paraphernalia and Magickal Weapons have varying levels of energy stored in them. This is because you've been sending energy through them or at them. You also have a certain amount of energy stored up in your body at any given moment. The key in magick, and especially in psychic self-defense, is not to rely on the energy stored in your body or in these magickal tools. What little energy is stored is rapidly depleted when used in psychic self-defense. It is not a good thing to wear yourself out in the midst of a psychic attack. You do not want to draw the energy or chi out of yourself. You want to draw it from the universe around you. That way you are not limited to the reserves of energy stored in you. This is a mistake that beginners commonly make. Under attack they switch to their inner reserves and quickly run their "batteries" dry. What I'd rather see you do is use the principle To Keep Silent to identify currents of energy out there in the universe around you, and let that flow through you. I'll speak more about this in the chapter on using energy.

As I mentioned earlier, I've listed the mind as a Lesser Magickal Weapon of Spirit. It is the mind that allows you to utilize all five principles of Magickal Artillery. It is the mind that knows. It is the mind that dares. It is the mind that imagines. Will is the power of the mind. Of all the Lesser Magickal Weapons, mind is the most important.

My defensive magick is "hermetic." It utilizes mental, psychic, and spiritual development and dispenses with magickal paraphernalia as much as possible. Others may surround themselves with magickal accessories. I use whatever is at hand and most often nothing other than what I came into the world with. You may begin your practice of magickal self-defense with ritual paraphernalia and Magickal Weapons, but it is likely that as your skill improves you will find yourself relying on such things less and less.

Magickal Weapons and ritual paraphernalia are training aids for beginners. You can think of them as training wheels on a bicycle. Ultimately we strive to achieve the mastery that will allow us to lay these tools aside and do without them.

Now that you've learned the importance and effects of will and discipline, as well as the proper use of Magickal Weapons, it is time to move on. There is one more element of Magickal Artillery that we have to examine before I discuss how to use energy: the imagination.

Imagination

FIVE

Imagination

If you want to know what a person is like, look at their Gods.

—Kerr Cuhulain

The human mind can conceive of any number of threats to project upon another person. As long as the aggressor can summon up enough power to send and/or manifest the threat, the possibilities are limitless. This may sound very frightening, but you can take comfort in the following two key principles of psychic self-defense:

- What the imagination has made, the imagination can unmake; and
- That which is thought into existence by someone's imagination can be thought out of existence by your imagination.

The first principle above is simply the first rule of magick restated: you create your own reality. In order to do this, you must develop the ability to clearly visualize your objectives.

"Man is an imagining being."[45] This is why one of the principles of Magickal Artillery is To Imagine. Dr. Jeffry Palmer puts it this way: "Becoming aware of the power of your own thoughts is the most important step in understanding how to handle the adverse influence of the negative thought of others."[46]

In magickal self-defense it is vital to be able to accurately visualize your goal. Your assailant is often acting from a distance, so being able to visualize your assailant is crucial. To Imagine is to set your sights on the target of your Magickal Artillery. If you can't imagine the target, you're going to miss your mark. If you haven't carefully considered exactly what you want and/or have not been able to accurately visualize your goal, then what you get will probably not meet your expectations or requirements. So an accurate and creative imagination is essential to defensive magick.

The more vivid your visualization, the more effective your magick will be. Dr. Jonn Mumford, a Western doctor trained in Eastern medicine and yoga, created the acronym CASE[47] to describe the various aspects of imagination essential to magick; the acronym stands for *Color, Action, Size, and Emotion*. I discussed the use of the CASE system in my book *Full Contact Magick*. Visualize your target in the most vivid colors that you can. Imagine your target in motion. If your target is a person, make them move. Make them bigger than life. Infuse their image with your emotion.

You must give careful consideration to what it is that you need to imagine in order for your magick to work. For example, when doing protective magick, you should always work

---

45. Gaston Bachelard, *The Poetics of Reverie* (1960), ch. 2, sect. 10.

46. Jeffry R. Palmer, PhD, "The Nature of Thought Energy," Project Sanctuary (accessed 12 October 2007).

47. Dr. Jonn Mumford, "Creative Visualization" audiotape. Date unknown.

with positive images rather than negative ones. Doing so will help to keep your focus clear and give you better results. For example, if I said to you, "Do not think of your enemy," your subconscious would automatically conjure up an image of your enemy so that you could see what it is I *don't* want you to see. Therefore, thoughts such as "Be safe" and "Be healthy" will work better than "No more danger." The former will get you thinking about safety and health. The latter will conjure up examples of danger in your mind. If you want to set up psychic defenses for yourself, it is best to imagine the strength of your wards and shields and your security within them.

In your meditation sessions, practice imagining different objects using the CASE system. Close your eyes and imagine each object in vivid (even nonsensical) colors. Make the object move. Have it rotate or flip over. Imagine each object several times its normal size. Put as much emotion into these exercises as you can.

Once you have mastered these simple exercises you must move on to the ability to visualize with your eyes open. It isn't a good idea to close your eyes in a defensive situation in order to visualize your target. You can do this in stages. Rather than closing your eyes, try covering them. Rub your hands together to warm them up. Cup your palms over your eyes and stare into the darkness thus created without closing your eyes. Imagine the same objects floating before you in this darkness. Doing this exercise gets you used to the idea of visualizing things with open eyes. Once you are able to master this, try doing this exercise with your eyes uncovered and open. Make the object so real that you feel you can touch it, taste it, and smell it. Put it on the table or grass in front of you.

Another useful exercise is to close your eyes and imagine the room or outdoor setting in which you are meditating.

Imagine what the room or yard around you looked like before you closed your eyes. Take a mental tour of the room or yard and examine the objects in it, one by one. Once you feel that you have examined each object thoroughly, open your eyes to check the objects. See how close you were in your visualization. Once you have mastered this exercise, close your eyes and imagine that you are getting up and walking into another room or into another part of the yard. Examine everything around you. Eventually you can progress to the point at which you are leaving your house or yard and moving around your neighborhood.

Defending the Astral Temple

One of the concepts I've discussed in my previous Warrior books is that of the astral temple, the psychic equivalent of the magick Circle (which I will discuss in chapter 11). An astral temple is the sacred space that you create entirely within your own mind. People use astral temples to connect with aspects of the divine. The astral temple is an inner place of refuge you can retreat to in your mind in order to recharge yourself. Astral temples may be private spaces or shared between members of covens or groups. I describe the process of creating them in *Full Contact Magick*. They are a product of your imagination and can be set up any way you or your group wants. Their architectural inspirations can be Egyptian, classical Greek acropolis, or Iron Age standing stones.

Why create such an astral temple? One reason is that it serves as a link between your conscious mind and your subconscious. I often go to my astral temple to encounter aspects of deity; I find them there waiting for me. Sometimes I find tokens or symbols that they have left for me to find. One might find messages from other Wiccans. These will help you to identify the things you need to work on in your life. What occurs in this astral temple resonates through your world and can manifest in it.

As you create your astral temple in your imagination, you also create its defenses in your imagination. If you have already created an astral temple for yourself, use whatever meditation you commonly use in order to go there. If you haven't, use one of my exercises from *Full Contact Magick* to make an astral temple for yourself. You are taking a journey inward to a special place where you will create this astral temple.

Of course, one of the places that a psychic attack could manifest is in this astral temple. If you are there, you must use the following techniques to defend yourself. If you are not, you should still be able to detect the attack. Because the astral temple was created by your mind, it is connected to your mind. If something tries to invade the temple or touch it in any way, you should be able to sense it instantly.

The defenses that you create in your mind for your astral temple can be made to look like battlements and fortifications. If this helps you imagine the perimeters of this magickal place, then put up as many walls as you need, instantly. Use any structure from any time period that is comfortable for you. You may prefer to imagine the psychic wards around your astral temple as crystal walls or as walls of light.

You don't need to have a doorway in the walls or wards of your astral temple. You don't need to worry about the doorway through which you entered this astral space. You only have to think of your astral temple and it will reappear for you. This "disappearing door" concept can help you to make the walls of your astral temple impregnable. Another useful technique for creating a temple with no "doors" is to use the "mist" technique that I described in *Full Contact Magick*. Close your eyes and imagine that you are standing in moonlight in front of a dark body of water. Imagine cold mist rising from the water. This is astral mist. Imagine the mist enveloping you. The mist transforms your surroundings, and when it dissipates you find yourself in your psychic temple. This is the sort of image that Marion Zimmer Bradley invoked in her book *The Mists of Avalon*: To get to the blessed isle you had to journey on a barge through the magickal mists. To come back, you simply imagine the mists enveloping you again and returning you to the mundane world.

In creating and defending an astral temple, visualization is crucial. Remember not to restrict your visualization of this space to your sense of sight. Involve all of your senses. You should not only see an image of your defensive walls or wards and be able to touch them, but you should also hear sounds echo off of them and you should smell the warm stone or brick.

You can place as many Magickal Weapons as you wish in these astral temples. Like their physical equivalent, these imaginary Magickal Weapons are focusing tools that you can use to focus your energy. Remember what I said earlier? What the imagination has made, the imagination can unmake. That which is thought into existence by someone's imagination can be thought out of existence by your imagination. Whatever comes at you, you are capable of arming yourself with whatever you need to deal with it. Give yourself a flaming sword, silver armor and a shield, a sharp spear, a powerful bow, whatever you need to defend you. There are no limits to what you can do. Use any of the shielding techniques that I will show you in chapter 11. Once you've gained control, get back to your waking state of consciousness and use the techniques that I've taught you on the physical plane to ensure that there won't be any further problems.

If a particular defensive construct that you have created doesn't work as well as you'd like, you can always add on to it. Real castles are frequently built upon the foundations of older ones. Astral temples work the same way. Try out different configurations until you find one that you are comfortable with. Experiment and see what works best for your situation. As with dreaming, it is a good idea to have your journal or Book of Shadows handy so that you can record what you've done and how it is working for you. Memories of trips into this astral world can fade quickly, as you're working in another state of consciousness. Memory does not work there the same way as it does in waking consciousness.

The astral temple can be used as a safe and defensible meeting place for several people who aren't able to meet physically. At a prearranged time, you and several others can meditate wherever you happen to find yourself and meet with the others in your astral temple. This is a form of astral projection.

While anyone can create something negative in their mind to throw at you, you can take control of that negative creation with your mind. Ralph Waldo Emerson called the imagination "an arm or weapon of the interior energy; only the precursor of the reason."[48] To Imagine is both the ability to clearly visualize your objective and the ability to conceive of a solution to your problems. It encompasses imagination and creativity. This of course indicates that you can work upon the imagination of your assailant. Making yourself fearful to your opponent will certainly affect their ability to attack you. Fear can be very unnerving to an enemy and can put them off. Be careful with this one. If it causes panic attacks in people around you, it can create some hazardous situations.

---

48. Ralph Waldo Emerson, "Books," *Society and Solitude*, 180.

You've now learned that what the imagination has made, the imagination can unmake. You've discovered that which is thought into existence by someone's imagination can be thought out of existence by your imagination. Now that we've spoken of awareness, will, and imagination, we can move on to the subject of energy. The first thing to understand when working with energy is the quantum principle of entanglement. We'll look at this principle in the next chapter.

Interconnection/Entanglement

six

Interconnection/Entanglement

Whatever happened to one particle would thus immediately
affect the other particle, wherever in the universe it may be.
Einstein called this "Spooky action at a distance."

—Amir D. Aczel, *Entanglement*

I n 1935, Albert Einstein, Boris Podolsky, and Nathan Rosen
published an article revealing the existence of quantum
entanglement. They described pairs of "entangled" photons,
connected by a mysterious link. It makes no difference how far
apart these entangled protons are. Even if they are light years
apart, if you were to measure the polarization of one of them,
you could instantly infer the polarity of the other. Please note:
you don't know the polarity of either particle *until you observe
one of them*. Thus the process of observing, or will, plays a part.

This all seemed impossible and illogical, since this process
was instantaneous. It was assumed at that time that the information could not travel between the two photons faster than

the speed of light. The problem was, this new theory of quantum mechanics very accurately predicted many of the discoveries in atomic physics and accurately described the "mechanics" involved. This "EPR paradox," as they called it, upset Einstein, who referred to it as "spooky action at a distance." We now know that while light and other signals cannot travel faster than the speed of light, the space of the universe is expanding in many places faster than the speed of light. The dimension of space isn't limited by the speed of light.

In 1964, physicist John Bell tried to prove that this entanglement was impossible. Bell proposed a mathematical inequality, which, if confirmed experimentally, would prove Einstein right and quantum physics wrong. However, if Bell's inequality were violated, then quantum entanglement would be proven to exist. Bell wasn't able to come up with an experimental proof, however.

Ten years later, Alain Aspect, building on the work of John Clauser and others, began research that would lead to the development of polarizers whose settings could be changed every ten nanoseconds. This allowed Aspect to set up a source of entangled photons. In 1982, Aspect, along with Philippe Grangier, Gérard Roger, and Jean Dalibard, showed clear violation of Bell's inequalities in conditions closely resembling the ideal "Gedanken experiment," which was the foundation of quantum theories. Quantum mechanics was vindicated and entanglement conclusively proved.[49]

This connection and instantaneous exchange of information regardless of separation distance is the "spooky action at

---

49. Alain Aspect, "Three Experimental Tests of Bell Inequalities by the Measurement of Polarization Correlations Between Photons," http://perso.orange.fr/eric.chopin/epr/aspect.htm (accessed 24 March 2007). "Experimental Tests of Bell's Inequality," http://www.mtnmath.com/whatrh/node81.html (accessed 24 March 2007).

a distance" that Einstein didn't like. He couldn't see the logic in it. It drove him crazy. It drove my editor crazy when she read my first draft of this book. She felt that "the logic doesn't work" and that "they were observing [this] because they are scientists experimenting." She even described it in almost the same way Einstein did, calling it "weird laws of physics." If you hold to the Newtonian worldview, this entanglement business certainly looks weird. It defies Newtonian logic. The thing is, this new quantum view allows us to explain many previously unexplained phenomena, both in physics and in psychic fields. Modern quantum mechanics is a completely different worldview than the old Newtonian one.

The most famous proof of the effect of observation on the outcome is in the classic "double slit" wave interference experiment known to every university physics student. When you fire electrons at a screen, you get a typical distribution pattern, just as you'd get if you fired marbles at a screen. However, strange things start to happen if you place a shield with two slits in it between the electron projector and the screen. When you fire electrons at a screen with the double slit shield in front of it, instead of getting the expected distribution pattern, *you get a wave interference pattern on the screen.* Suddenly the electron particles are behaving like waves. This is exactly what Schrödinger's wave equation describes. These particles cannot be described as particles. They behave as waves and can only accurately be described by a wave function.

In an attempt to discover what was happening, scientists next modified this dual slit experiment, placing a recording device next to this shield to see which slit the electrons they were firing actually went through.[50] To everyone's intense sur-

---

50. "Young Two-Slit Experiment," http://zebu.uoregon.edu/~js/21st
     _century_science/lectures/lec13.html (accessed 24 March 2007).

prise, the electrons stopped behaving like a wave and started behaving like particles in the presence of the recording device, creating the original distribution pattern instead of a wave interference pattern. The inescapable conclusion: the act of observation affects the outcome. This experiment has been replicated thousands of times since. As I noted earlier, all systems exist simultaneously in all quantum mechanically possible states until an observer interacts to "collapse" the "state vector" by making an observation. The state vector fully specifies any quantum mechanical state in which a quantum mechanical system can exist. In other words, the state vector is the total possible states that could occur, the total potential of the situation—the act of observation, the will of the observer, that causes the "state vector" to "collapse" into reality. You choose one of those possible states and cause it to become real. In other words, you create your own reality.

So right now you're probably saying to yourself: "OK. So what? What has this got to do with magick and psychic self-defense?"

Everything.

As I mentioned at the beginning of this book, one of the oldest concepts in Celtic mythology is the idea that everything is interconnected. One of the cornerstones of the science of quantum physics is the concept of entanglement. Experiments have proved, again and again, that on the level of the Planck scale, everything *is* connected.

One of the aspects of the concept of entanglement is the principle of superposition, which is a consequence of Schrödinger's wave equation that I told you about earlier. Superposition tells us that a single particle of matter (in other words, a single wave form) can be in multiple places at once. This has actually been photographed by researchers in recent years, and you can see examples of these photos on the Internet.[51] A single particle can be seen at two separate points and up to as many as three thousand locations in the same instant. This isn't three thousand parts of a single particle; it's three thousand separate locations for a *single wave function, a single particle*. This phenomenon is directly linked to Schrödinger's particle/wave duality. Scientists refer to such states as Bose-Einstein condensates. The unified field at the Planck level that I mentioned earlier is what makes this amazing potentiality possible.

An understanding of the nature of these entanglements is developing rapidly. Dr. Dean Radin, in his book *Entangled Minds*, shows us that this idea can be extended out into what he calls *bioentanglement*, or entanglement in living systems. Experiments are already proving bioentanglement to be a fact. For example, a study was conducted at the University of Milan in which human neurons were grown in a dish that had electrical contacts underneath these neurons.[52] Then, from the same batch of cells, scientists grew them in another identical dish. The idea was that if those neurons, coming from the same source, are actually connected (even though they appear to be in separate dishes), then if one stimulates the neurons in one dish, one should find a reaction in the other dish.

The researchers then stimulated the neurons in one dish with certain light frequencies, using a laser. A laser was used

---

51. Jean-Francois Colonna, "From the Infinitely Small to the Infinitely Big," http://www.lactamme.polytechnique.fr/Mosaic/descripteurs/Galerie _FromTheInfinitelySmallToTheInfinitelyBig.FV.html (accessed 15 March 2000); Jean-Francois Colonna (15 March 2000), "Gallery: Quantum Mechanics," http://www.lactamme.polytechnique.fr/Mosaic/descripteurs/Galerie _QuantumMechanics.FV.html (20 December 1994). "Tridimensional Display of the Dynamics of a Linear Superposition of 6 Eigenstates of the Hydrogen Atom," http://www.lactamme.polytechnique.fr/Mosaic/images/ HYDR.91.16.D/display.html (accessed 22 October 2007).

52. Dean Radin, PhD, in *What the Bleep!?: Down the Rabbit Hole* (DVD, 2006).

since laser light can be easily blocked from affecting the neurons in the nonstimulated dish. The researchers put the nonstimulated dish in a light-tight box away from the stimulated dish. They made sure there was no way that the laser, even a single photon from that laser, could hit the nonstimulated dish. They then stimulated the first batch of neurons. A large electrical reaction was recorded in the nonstimulated neurons in the box. This experiment has been repeated with various refinements and with identical results.

Experiments such as this one help us to understand previously unexplainable psychic phenomena. Suddenly we have an explanation, a connection that explains how this information can flow from one to another. Modern quantum physics has given rise to the concepts of quantum teleportation (instant transfer of information from one place to another) and quantum encryption (information recorded in the unified field at the Planck level). It explains the information connections that make ESP and remote viewing possible, and provides explanations for phenomena such as hauntings (more on this in a later chapter).

At the Planck level, the unified field is the coarse fabric from which everything in our universe is manifested. This unified field, also called the zero point field, state vector, or quantum wave function, is a wave consisting of all possible shapes. Physicist Nikola Tesla came up with the idea of the unified field[53] in his efforts to establish a theory that reconciled the general theory of relativity with electromagnetism—that grand Theory of Everything that I mentioned at the beginning of this book. The

53. Peter Hickman, "A Unified Field Theory," (31 October 1999), http://homepage.ntlworld.com/peter.hickman1/ (accessed 3 November 2007). Kurt Reichling, "An Essay on the Relativistic Theory of the Non-Symmetric Field," (1 September 2006, © Kurt Reichling), http://e-kr.org/ (accessed 3 November 2007).

unified field is not a wave of matter. The unified field is a state of infinite, abstract potentiality. It is a wave of consciousness. The play and display of information at this basement level of existence creates everything. The unified field is the simultaneous existence of all possible states, which consciousness transforms into the universe we experience. Magick is the process of manipulating this potentiality. This intangible world creates the tangible world.

Everything in life is made up of energy. Even the things around us that we consider to be "solid" material are just energy. Atoms consist mostly of empty space. If you imagine the nucleus of a hydrogen atom to be the size of a basketball, then its electron is orbiting twenty miles away. It is our perception of matter that makes all this empty space seem "solid."

We are made up of this same energy. It flows through us. We are connected to the world around us by this unified field, this energetic link, though as yet few people in our modern society are aware of this connection. This unified field resonates throughout our reality, allowing energy exchange at a quantum level.

Quantum theory tells us that matter can be viewed not as "solid," but as waves of probability. We know that waves can combine and interfere with other waves. Thus we can treat two particles interacting in wavelike terms as the creation of a new, more complex wave. Not two waves, but one wave. In other words, these two particles can no longer be considered separate. Quantum mathematics predict that if you have one particle that splits into two, or two particles that interact, once those particles separate they are not really separate. Both particles contain some aspect of each other. This means that ever since the Big Bang, everything has been connected to everything else.

As the double slit experiment and others that have followed it clearly show, it is possible to use your will to influence this "collapse." Obviously there are many variables involved, some very strong, so the effect of your will can vary. One common scenario that people often throw at me is winning the lottery with magick. If what you say is true, they insist, then if I directed my will at the lottery, I should win it. This is true, but you must take into account the fact that millions of other people are desperately and intensely directing their desires, their will, at winning that same lottery. There are a lot of wills tugging that event in many different directions. You'd need a very strong will indeed to overcome all of that.

On the other hand, when I've directed my will at situations in my life to enhance prosperity (other than lotteries), my magick has always worked to one extent or another. In such situations I'm the only one exerting my influence on the situation, so it is much more likely to turn out the way I want it to. Another consideration is that if you did win the lottery, you'd invariably find out that the way the universe works to balance things would usually throw expenses at you to use up your windfall that you didn't have before. It's all about finding balance.

Power Over versus Mastery

Occidental ceremonial magick is all about using ritual to control energies or entities outside of the magician's Circle. It is about dominating someone or something. This is a concept that Starhawk labeled *power over*. But that's not the way I approach magick, and especially not magickal self-defense. The Warrior's power is *power with*. Remember what I said earlier about magickal self-defense being an internal process? To effectively defend yourself magickally, you need to harmonize or entrain yourself with the universe surrounding you. This universe all exists on one level, overlapping. You need to become a valve or gateway through which the energy flows to where you want it to go.

The person attacking you likely believes in *power over* and likely treats magick as an external process. If they didn't, they wouldn't be attacking you. Those who launch magickal attacks typically treat magickal power like chattel: something to possess. This is a weakness that you can exploit.

The magickal energy that you and I use doesn't belong to us or anyone else. We're all simply tapping into the vast universe around us. Remember what I said about Magickal Weapons? They only contain so much power. You can only stockpile so many. In reality, you don't have to stockpile energy at all. Magickal self-defense is all about learning to use more effectively the power available to everyone. Power isn't something you own; it is something that you achieve. Master yourself, and everything else takes care of itself. True magickal power comes from within you. If you want to defend yourself, you only need to look inside of yourself and find that magickal power that is in each of us.

Entrainment and Resonance

What implications do entanglement and wave functions have for ancient concepts of psychic self-defense? In the introduction I mentioned that one of the oldest principles states that any attack that cannot reach the subconscious mind will fail. Yet quantum entanglement shows us that we are all already inextricably connected. If we are already interconnected, how can we hope to stave off an attack on our subconscious?

Psychic attack and defense isn't about connecting or dominating as much as it is about:

- Finding the right connection, and
- Causing the person at the end of that connection to entrain or resonate the way you want them to.

Everything around you rises in waves of vibration from the unified field at the Planck level of existence, becoming energy and particles that we experience. Sensing and manipulating the potentiality at this level to create these vibrations is the basis of magick. The vibrations or oscillations of two objects affect one another, and we can use this principle, called *entrainment*, in psychic self-defense and magick.

Entrainment is the process whereby two connected oscillating systems, having similar periods, fall into synchrony. The system with the greater frequency slows down, and the system with the lesser frequency accelerates until both systems are oscillating with the same frequency. Physicist Christiaan Huygens coined the term *entrainment* in 1666 after he noticed that two pendulum clocks had moved into the same swinging rhythm. Subsequent experiments duplicated this process. Entrainment occurs because small amounts of energy are transferred between the two systems when they are out of phase in such a way as to produce negative feedback. As these systems synchronize in phase, the amounts of energy gradually reduce to zero. In the realm of physics, entrainment appears to be related to resonance.

Nature is full of examples of resonance. Examples include the acoustic resonances of musical instruments, the tidal resonance of the Bay of Fundy, orbital resonance as exemplified by some moons of our solar system's giant gas planets, the resonance of the basilar membrane in the human ear, and resonance in electrical circuits.

A resonant object, whether mechanical, acoustic, or electrical, will probably have more than one resonant frequency. It will be easy to vibrate at those frequencies, and more difficult to vibrate at other frequencies. It will tend to vibrate at this resonant frequency when energy is applied to it. Quantum is the energy required to move from one resonant state to another. This is where the ideas of quantum physics originated. In effect, the object filters out all frequencies other than its resonance.

Whenever someone launches a psychic attack at you in some way, they are latching onto the connection with you and affecting your "polarity." Often this works through one of your faults or weaknesses and often through a weakness of the attacker. It is the polarity or resonance working through this link that creates the problems for you. Simply put: the attacker forces you into synchrony with their negative energy.

There are countless references to this in old books of magick and psychic phenomena, which refer to vibrations. The German jazz historian Joachim-Ernst Berendt once said: "(a) since the one sure thing we can say about fundamental matter is that it is vibrating, and (b) since all vibrations are theoretically sound, then (c) it is not unreasonable to suggest that the universe is music and should be perceived as such."[54] The magickal power of song is a very old concept. A mythical example of this magickal power of words in song is in the epic Finnish poem, the Kalevala. In it, the God Väinämöinen transforms Joukahainen, who had angered him, into part of the landscape simply by singing.

In my earlier Warrior books I described mantras. Mantras are a concept from Eastern magickal philosophy. The word *mantra* comes from a Sanskrit root that means to "think or reason." Mantras are a way of verbalizing thought energy. It is this philosophy that gave us the ancient idea that knowing the correct name for a thing gives you power over it. This is a vital part of the concept of mantras: once you know the real name of a thing, you can create it by its sound.

---

54. Mickey Hart, *Drumming at the Edge of Magic* (New York: HarperSanFrancisco, 1990), 119.

In Eastern philosophy there are several key principles involving mantras:

- *Varna*—The concept of varna holds that sound is eternal and that every letter of the alphabet is a deity. Thus, words become words of power. This is similar to Hebrew Cabalistic numerology systems or Norse runes, which assign power to each letter of the alphabet. This is also the basis of the ceremonial magician's grimoires, which list words and names of power.

- *Nada*—Every entity has a germ sound (in the sense of germination) called *nada*, which creates it out of the void. The Hindus consider nada to be the heart of creation. The best known example is the well-known mantra usually written as *OM*, which is actually the triphthong *AUM*. The *A* stands for *Agni*, or Fire, and is also related to the god Vishnu. *U* stands for *Varuna*, or Water, and is related to Shiva. The *M* stands for *Marut*, or Air, and is related to Brahma. Thus, by chanting "AUM" you are invoking this trinity of deities.

- *Dharanis*—These are single phrases, sometimes called *satya-vacana*, which refer to the solemn uttering of a great truth. An example of using a dharani to invoke deities is the chant used by the Krishna Consciousness movement. It goes like this: "Hare Krishna, Hare Krishna, Krishna, Krishna, Hare Hare; Hare Rama, Hare Rama, Rama Rama, Hare, Hare." *Hare* means "Hail" and Krishna and Rama are deities in the Hindu pantheon.

Lest you think that this concept is foreign to Western culture, just look at the practices of the Christian church. Common mantras in Catholic churches include choruses of "Hallelujah," Hail Marys, and the well-known phrase "In the Name of the

Father, and of the Son, and of the Holy Spirit." By saying these words, Catholics expect to invoke this power. But of course, as many a Catholic theologian will tell you, there is no magick in Catholicism!

You may already be familiar with these concepts, as the use of chanting, toning, and song to raise energy are common practices in modern Paganism. The simplest technique is toning, in which a single syllable sound is repeatedly chanted in order to raise energy. Toning stimulates the flow of energy in you, but more importantly, it permits you to get your objective to resonate with you through the principle of entrainment. In *Full Contact Magick* I described toning techniques and their effects. If you've never heard of toning, it works like this: Each person in a group takes a deep breath and then sings the chosen tone until they run out of breath. They then quickly take another breath and repeat the tone. Because different people are running out of breath at different times, the sound of the group's mantra should be more or less continuous. Start with a low pitch. As each person feels the energy start to rise, they raise their voice an octave in pitch, and/or increase the volume. All watch the person directing the group. This leader will use some sort of agreed signal like raising their arms to indicate when the energy has peaked. This will occur at a point where the tone sounds and feels "right." When the signal is given, all of the participants stop toning and direct the energy raised to wherever it is required.

After a while you will easily come to recognize when the energy has peaked. It is the moment when all of the people in the group are in perfect resonance—the point when everyone is in synchrony, when everyone is on exactly the same frequency. It is an unmistakable feeling. This is when it feels "right." You are all vibrating together, linked by the energy.

Different mantras or tones have different effects. If your energy is depleted, try toning the well-known mantra "AUM" for a few minutes. This will draw energy into you, and is most useful if you are trying to recharge yourself after a magickal attack. To expel excess or negative energy, try chanting the mantra "MA" (pronounced as in grandMA) while imagining the negative energy passing out of you. This mantra helps the negative energy to flow out of you. You can also use "MA" to send healing energy out of yourself to assist another person. The only difference is the intent that you attach to it.

One very useful mantra that I use all the time to energize myself or to help direct energy is the mantra "HA." Take three sharp breaths in and then shout "HA!" Do this a few times and see how you feel. It is a very useful technique if you find your reserves depleted. Readers who are martial artists will recognize this mantra as the shout or "kiai" or "heit" that accompanies a punch or kick. If uttered at the moment of contact, it helps to release the chi. In Kendo, calls known as "katsu" are used with upward stabbing moves and calls known as "totsu" with striking motions. Ever notice how a weight lifter will yell while completing an especially heavy lift? It's the same principle at work.

If you are under a lot of stress, you tend to tense up and, as I mentioned earlier, tension can inhibit the flow of energy. One mantra you can use to relieve tension is called *Bhramari breathing*. Bhramari breathing slows your breathing and heart rate quite rapidly. Part of the reason this works is that it mimics snoring, a sound you usually make when asleep. This triggers the same sort of relaxation response in your waking consciousness. Bhramari breathing can also be used to overcome and eliminate pain, especially migraines.

To do Bhramari breathing, sit in a comfortable position. Begin making a soft snoring sound as you exhale (with practice you can make this sound while inhaling, too). It does not have to be loud; it should sound like a sigh or a groan. Start with a low pitch and with each breath raise up through an octave until it feels right to you. Continue until you feel like making a big sigh. It takes about twenty exhalations to arrive at this point. This big sigh signals that the exercise has worked.

A similar technique in Chi Kung uses a hissing "shsss" mantra. You softly blow on a wound while making this hissing sound. Doing so can dramatically reduce the pain of the wound, and can even help it heal. Frequencies between 20 to 50 Hz have been found to strengthen human bones and help them grow. This is the frequency range in which cats purr, which may account for why they seem to have remarkable powers of recuperation.[55]

Now let's look at some of the many frequencies that resonate in the human body. As I mentioned earlier, in recent times brain connectivity has become one of the most influential concepts in cognitive neuroscience. The focus in cognitive neuroscience has gradually shifted in emphasis from studies of functional segregation to studies of functional integration. As our examination of ancient practices such as mantras and Bhramari breathing suggest, brainwave synchronization or entrainment can be achieved by exposing the human brain to specific audio frequencies. This causes a response directly related to the frequency of the signal introduced, called binaural beats. Two tones close in frequency generate a beat frequency at the difference of the frequencies, which is generally subsonic. For example, a 500 Hz tone and 510 Hz tone will produce a subsonic 10 Hz tone, roughly in the middle of the alpha range. The resulting subsonic tone affects the state of mind of the subject.

---

55.   David Harrison, "Cats' Purring Linked to Old Wives' Tale of Their Nine Lives," *National Post* (Toronto), 20 March 2001.

Let's look at the effects of brainwave synchronization and the resulting brain waves and mind states. These are the results of the following frequencies:

- Gamma: 26–80 Hz. Results in higher mental activity, including perception, problem-solving, fear, and consciousness. In some studies these frequencies have been linked to ESP ability, heightened insight, and out-of-body experiences, or OBEs.

- Beta: 12Hz–38Hz. Further divided into three categories: SMR, beta 1, and beta 2.
  - › SMR (12Hz–15Hz) Results in relaxed focus and improved attention.
  - › Beta 1 (15Hz–20Hz) Increases mental abilities, IQ, and focus.
  - › Beta 2 (20Hz–38Hz) Results in anxiousness and a heightened sense of alertness.

- Alpha: 8Hz - 12Hz. Results in a state where the brain is awake, but not processing much. This can be a useful frequency for meditation. It is also associated with a feeling of being "connected," dreaming (REM sleep), and states of creative reverie.

- Theta: 3Hz–8Hz. Associated with the hypnogogic state right after you wake up or begin to fall asleep (drowsiness). It can be useful in self-hypnosis.
  - › Theta 1 (3Hz–5Hz) suppression can result in improved concentration and attention while reducing hyperactivity (after the session).
  - › Theta 2 (5Hz–8Hz) Results in a very relaxed sleep. This frequency range is often related to paranormal/spiritual experiences.
  - › The first Schumann resonance (7.83 Hz—a spectrum peak in the ELF portion of the earth's

electromagnetic field spectrum) Associated with the hypnogogic state, out-of-body experiences, and various hormonal releases.

- Delta: 0.2–3Hz. This frequency range usually results in deep sleep.

Some studies have shown that these frequencies help in treating certain medical conditions.

I've heard many arguments that sound or music deters psychic attack. One source I examined suggested continuous playing of Christmas carols, nursery rhymes, or religious music as a psychic defense. The vibrations and harmonies of classical music are said by some to repel negative influences. For example, Robert Bruce reports that "I have yet to find a [psychic attack] that could stay active while the William Tell Overture, and other such stimulating pieces, are played at high volume."[56]

Music may be used to drown out the symptoms of psychic attack. Music may soothe the victim. But music by itself doesn't act as a shield. There are a lot of different frequencies in even a simple piece of music. What I'm talking about in my discussion of resonance is a single frequency, not a collection of different sounds. A single frequency can cause a thing to achieve the resonance you desire. Music cannot.

A variation on this idea is the ancient practice of using percussion to "drive away demons." Drumming is certainly an excellent way to raise energy for defense and to bolster the spirits of the defenders. I've also heard it suggested that wind chimes are a passive countermeasure. Wind chimes certainly help stir up the chi and may soothe the victim, but they aren't a

---

56. Robert Bruce, "Developing Natural Resistance to the Negatives of Life," http://www.astraldynamics.com/tutorials/?BoardID=10&BulletinID=215 (accessed 12 October 2007).

defense by themselves. Toning or playing a particular frequency certainly *can* help you establish the resonance that you need to work the connections that link you with the psychic assailant. You can see from our discussion that it is how the audio vibrations cause entrainment in your mind that causes certain mental states. This provides a base state from which you can work your defensive magick. Having achieved this base state, it is time to move energy to actually defend yourself. Moving energy is what we will discuss in the next chapter.

Energy

SEVEN

Energy

The physical body may be trapped in a situation with no realistic alternative. But the mind and spirit can never be trapped.

—Robert Bruce[57]

Learning how to detect and manipulate energy is essential to psychic self-defense. There are basically two forms of psychic attack:

- Operating through thought-forms. I will touch upon this in a later chapter on the subject of ghosts and artificial elementals.
- Utilizing the currents or force of energy/chi.

This chapter will focus on utilizing the currents or force of energy.

As I pointed out in my book *Full Contact Magick*, working with your own energy familiarizes you with its "feel." Basically, you are becoming aware of the specific resonances that your body has as well as the resonance of things that commonly surround you. This makes it easier to detect energy from other

---

57. Robert Bruce, "Developing Natural Resistance to the Negatives of Life."

sources in your vicinity. That, in turn, makes it possible for you to banish unwanted energy that might be affecting you.

Energy feels different to each of us. In chapter 1, I showed you how different people experience different symptoms when experiencing a psychic attack. The same holds true when different people experience the flow of energy. When chi is flowing, some people feel heat or cold, some a pins-and-needles sensation, some a buzzing sensation. It is different for each of us. People feel energy in different parts of their body too: some feel a buzzing in their third eye, in their hands, feet, or in their solar plexus. Working with energy is the only way to discover how it feels for you.

As I pointed out earlier, you need to become sensitive to the currents of energy within and without you in order to be effective in magickal defense. You must sense the currents of energy around you that you need, connect to them, and let them flow through you, rather than relying on your physical reserves. I warned you of this earlier: if you only use the energy stored within you, your "batteries" will soon run out of "juice." There is no need for this to happen. You are in the midst of an omnipresent ocean of life energy. In magickal self-defense you make yourself a valve or a gateway to let this energy funnel through you in the direction that you direct it with your will.

Your personal energy levels are connected to seasonal variations in energy, which are important to keep in mind. For example, the vernal and autumnal equinoxes are traditionally considered to be times of turning of the tides of energy and times of astral storms. Knowing this information allows you to compensate for these disturbances or variations.

The problem that a lot of novices run into, especially if they are self-taught, is that they don't know what this flow of energy or chi feels like. The flow of chi (or ki) will feel a certain way to you. By practicing techniques from disciplines such as Chi Kung, you can get this chi or energy circulating in your body and familiarize yourself with its feel. Once you've experienced this feeling, you'll find it easier to access chi when you need it. You'll know when the energy is flowing in other energy techniques because you can detect when chi is flowing, having experienced it in another application. Awareness of the energy flow during magickal self-defense gives you a much better indication of how effective your defense is at the time you are using it.

Here's a simple exercise that will get the chi flowing in your body and quickly break up any obstructions to the flow of chi. Stand in the Entering Tranquility posture that I described to you in chapter 3, hands at your sides. Start shaking your hands from the wrist. Let the shaking move up to your elbows, then up to your shoulders, and then let your whole body shake with a big shiver from your head right down to your feet. Pause for a moment in stillness. Repeat this shaking process two more times. You should now feel a sensation throughout your body and quite intensely in the palms of your hands (which are sub-chakras). For some it will be a feeling of hot or cold, for others a feeling of pins and needles, or even a rushing sensation. What you are feeling is the flow of chi through your body. That sensation, whatever it is for you, is what you should feel every time that you raise energy or do magick. That's what chi feels like to you.

As I mentioned earlier, to defend yourself with magick you must focus energy at your target with your will. Using the Entering Tranquility posture that I described earlier, we can move into a number of different techniques to access magickal energy. In *Full Contact Magick*, I showed you how to collect energy between your palms or arms with a couple of exercises called Forming a Ball and Holding the Ball. Hold your palms a few inches apart in front of you without letting them touch one another or hold your arms in a circle in front of you as if you were clasping a beach ball to your chest. Imagine this energy forming a swirling ball of energy between your hands or between your arms and your chest. Use your will to cause those variables to collapse to make this ball of energy form. Let it gradually grow, pushing against your palms or arms. Once you are done with it, press it into your abdomen in the region of your navel and reabsorb it.

I have you press your ball of energy into your abdomen to reabsorb it because in Asian medicine and martial arts, this is an energy storage area. The area just behind and about three inches below the navel is known as the Dantian. There are four energy fields in the body in Chinese Chi Kung: Yuanguan, Dantian, Niyuan and Zhongyuan. To the martial artist and the magician, the Dantian is the most important. This energy storage area is the foundation of Tai Chi and Chi Kung practice.

If you find it difficult at first to form this ball of energy between your hands, try this: Standing in the Entering Tranquility posture, place your hands together and cup them as if to scoop up some water with them. Bring your cupped hands up in front of your face and blow into them. As you do so, imagine the energy forming between your hands. Feel the energy and heat cupped in your palms. Now hold your hands out as described earlier, facing but not touching, and let this energy grow between them. This is a useful "jump start" technique for beginners.

If you've used the exercises I've described so far, you will now be familiar with what chi feels like as it courses through you. You've gotten used to the idea of sending energy out through both of your hands and collecting it between them. One hand is naturally a "projective" hand: that is, you tend to send your energy out of this one hand. The other hand is said to be receptive: in other words, you tend to sense or draw in energy currents more easily with this hand. It is said that for right-handed people the right, or dominant, hand is the projective hand while the left hand is the receptor. In left-handed people, the reverse is true. All that is probably accurate for the untrained person. However, just as in martial arts you learn to strike with either the hand or the foot, you can train yourself to project or receive with either hand. You should practice using both hands in both receiving and sending energy.

Now I'm going to show you a technique for sending out defensive energy. I call it Pushing the Sky. Start in the Entering Tranquility posture, with your arms hanging relaxed at your sides. Turn your hands so that the palms face down and the fingers of each hand are turned inwards. Your hands will now be at right angles to your arms. Keeping the arms straight and hanging downward, swing your hands inward so that the tips of your fingers are almost but not quite touching. Pause and sense the currents in the earth beneath you. Imagine yourself putting down roots and connect with these currents.

Now, with your hands still at right angles and your arms straight, swing your arms in a continuous arc upward. As you do so, breathe in and imagine the energy flowing up into you. Pause with your hands over your head, fingers almost touching, hands still at right angles at the end of your straight arms, your head tilted slightly back. Hold your breath for a second. Then push upward, as if pushing the sky. Feel the energy release and flow out of your hands, as if you are pushing it out. Once you have released the energy, let your arms fall in an arc to your sides, hands now relaxed and hanging normally.

A similar technique that I'm quite fond of is called Pushing Mountains. This technique works particularly well for me with the Magickal Artillery concept. Start in the Entering Tranquility posture. Raise your hands to chest level at either side of you, elbows back, palms facing forward and fingers pointing up, as if you're about to push something in front of you. Sense the energy currents in the earth beneath you. Imagine yourself putting down roots and connect with these currents. Breathe in gently. Feel the energy rush up into you. Once the energy has built up, breathe out and push your hands forward, as if pushing a mountain away from you. Feel the energy flow out of your hands as you push it away. Let the energy stream freely from your hands. Once you've let the energy go, let your hands fall back to your sides and return to Entering Tranquility.

You can repeat either of these exercises as many times as you need to. Once you've sent off the energy that you need to with Pushing the Sky or Pushing Mountains, clench your fists and bring your fists briefly to your side, palms up. This helps to shut off the energy flow. Release your fists, return to the Entering Tranquility posture, and ground out any surplus energy.

Chakras

In *Full Contact Magick* I described the various chakras from Hindu and Tantric metaphysics. Chakras are the energy centers located along your spine. The reason that I mention them in a book of magickal self-defense relates to what I said earlier about the importance of keeping energy channels in your body free at all times. Knowing where the chakras are located, recognizing energy blocks at these chakras, and knowing how to free these blocks are essential to an effective magickal defense. From the lowest to the highest, the chakras are:

· *Muladhara*—The root chakra, located at the pelvic plexus between the anus and urethra. Chi or kundalini energy originates from this chakra. Energy blocks at this chakra can affect the ovaries and testes.

- *Swadhisthana*—Located at the hypogastric plexus behind the navel. This is the area known as the Dantian in Chi Kung. As I mentioned earlier, it is an energy storage area. Energy blocks at this chakra can affect the suprarenal glands.
- *Manipura*—Located at the solar plexus. Energy blocks at this chakra can affect the pancreas.
- *Anahata*—Located at the cardiopulmonary plexus in the spine at the level of the nipples. Energy blocks at this chakra affect the heart and circulatory system.
- *Vishuddha*—Located at a point in the spine opposite the larynx. Energy blocks at this chakra affect the pharyngeal plexus, thyroid, and parathyroids.
- *Ajna*—Located at the pineal gland in the head, roughly between the ears and straight back behind a point between the eyebrows referred to as the "third eye." Energy blocks at this location affect the pineal gland.
- *Sahasrara*—Located at the top of the head. Energy blocks at this location affect the mind.
- *Bindu* (also known as *Brahmarandra*)—This is the highest of the chakras, located at the point just to the rear of the crown of the head. This is known in Chi Kung as the baihui ("meeting of a hundred meridians"). It is considered to be an energy safety valve in Chi Kung.

Kundalini energy starts at the root chakra, Muladhara, and rises up through the spinal cord, which is known as *Sushumna*. The energy passes through each of the other chakras, energizing each in turn. When the energy arrives at the topmost chakra, Bindu, it then flows back down channels to either side of the spine called *ida* and *pingala*. If you notice problems in one of the parts of the body listed above, it is always a good idea to check for blockages in the related chakras.

One way to give yourself a "psychic energy check" is to activate each of these chakras, in sequence or separately. To start, place yourself in a relaxed posture such as Entering Tranquility. A horizontal position on your back is another option. Visualize breathing energy into each of your chakras, one at a time. Since the energy starts at Muladhara and rises up the spinal cord, it is best to start at Muladhara and work upward:

- *Muladhara*—Visualize this as a ball of *red* light. Once you sense that this chakra is activated, move on to...
- *Swadhisthana*—Visualize this as a ball of *orange* light. Once you sense that this chakra is activated, move on to...
- *Manipura*—Visualize this as a ball of *yellow* light. Once you sense that this chakra is activated, move on to...
- *Anahata*—Visualize this as a ball of *green* light. Once you sense that this chakra is activated, move on to...
- *Vishuddha*—Visualize this as a ball of *blue* light. Once you sense that this chakra is activated, move on to...
- *Ajna*—Visualize this as a ball of *violet* light. Once you sense that this chakra is activated, move on to...
- *Sahasrara*—Visualize this as a ball of *indigo* light. Once you sense that this chakra is activated, move on to...
- *Bindu*—Visualize this as a ball of *white* light.

If you detect a blockage at any one of these chakras, you can take a moment to activate it by visualizing the appropriately colored energy at that chakra. Blockages occurring at any of the chakras can affect this flow of energy as well as physical health. Each of the chakras is connected to certain systems in the body.

Your body also has subchakras, or secondary energy centers. For example, there are subchakras located in the palms and fingertips. You can send and receive sensory and energetic information through these subchakras. This is one of the reasons that I have been teaching you exercises requiring you to send and form energy with your hands. The energy naturally flows out of these subchakras.

Magick and Quantum Mechanics

Now that we've looked at some simple techniques for sensing and sending energy, let's take a fresh look the typical structure of a magickal ritual in light of our knowledge of quantum mechanics, to see what is really going on:

- Rituals often start with some sort of purification of one's mind, body, and surroundings. What you should be trying to do here is to free yourself of interfering resonances, cutting out the background "static" so that you can get a clear sense of your own energy "baseline" from which to operate.

- Rituals next move into a technique that allows the participants to achieve a nonlocalized state of consciousness. This is the process of becoming "silent" to sense the flow of energy around you. As I mentioned earlier, it also makes the random energy around you more coherent.

- Often, rituals require the participants to meditate on the elements (Earth, Air, Fire, Water, and Spirit). Doing so will help your mind to fully open your awareness in order to identify the streams of energy resonance that affect you or that you need to affect.

- Next, rituals require participants to invoke deities or entities that are to assist in the magick. Here you are reaching into your subconscious to identify with the archetypes that energize and inspire you, in preparation for manipulating energy with your will.

- Rituals ensure that the participants raise energy and focus it on the target of the work, connecting with the target. You create this energy through dance, drumming, toning, chanting, channeling energy with your will power, and so on. You're reaching out with your will, connecting with the appropriate resonance pattern, and you're now going to send energy out along this wave.

- Next, ritual participants visualize the desired result, helping to focus their will upon the work at hand. This creates a "resonant template" that helps collapse the multiple probabilities into the particular result they want to achieve. You release the energy into the target while strongly visualizing the target achieved (energizing the resonance in the target).

- Finally, ritual participants ground themselves. This disconnects you from the resonant link that you've established with your target.

Negative Energy Detection

Earlier in this chapter I showed you exercises for acquiring a feeling for your chi or energy as well as the energy that surrounds you. I've also shown you toning exercises in order to give you a feel for the resonance involved in energy work. Using this experience as a baseline, you can teach yourself to detect negative energy that has been directed at you. I've also mentioned the subchakras in your hands. Let's see how we can use these to detect energy.

I've shown you some exercises involving forming and directing energy with your hands. Training your hands to be receptive to energy is quite easy. By holding your hands over various parts of your body or someone else's, you can sense the flow of energy under the skin. With practice you will be able to locate "hot spots" that may indicate the presence of an injury or illness. Practice locating with your hands each of the chakras that I listed earlier. Sense the energy at each of these locations, starting at the bottom at Muladhara and working upward. You can often determine where an energy blockage is occurring using this technique. Once you have located the spot, you can use the same hand to reverse the flow and project healing energy into the site.

With practice you can develop the sensitivity in your hands to detect negative energy that is being directed at you. Holding your hands out from your body, you can slowly turn until you feel incoming energy. Doing so can help identify the source of a psychic attack. Animals seem to use this sense all the time. Notice how your pets react to energy that you project. Be alert if they start exhibiting this behavior at other times when you aren't using energy yourself. Animals are much more in tune with these subtle flows of energy than the average human in today's world. Their behavior can sometimes be an indication of a psychic attack in progress.

Another exercise is a variation on the Passing the Ball exercise that I described earlier: Take an object such as a crystal, marble, or rock and charge it with your energy. Pass it to the next person and have them note their sensations. Ask them to charge an object and pass it to you so that you can do the same. This helps develop those psychometric skills that I described earlier in this book. As you develop your practice you will come to learn that these are useful skills.

This sensitivity will ultimately allow you to identify the direction that a psychic attack is coming from. One way to do this starts with the Entering Tranquility posture. Close your eyes. Turn slowly clockwise in increments, pausing with both feet on the ground at each change. Sense the energy around you. You can hold your hands out in front of you to act as energy receptors if it helps you to do so. Once you feel the energy flow and can identify where it is coming from, take a moment to determine which way it is flowing. Is it incoming or outgoing? What does its resonance feel like? This will help you to decide on the procedure that you'll use to deal with it. Once you've finished, don't forget to ground and seal off the flow.

Vampirism

Psychic vampires were first mentioned in the Flying Rolls (instructional texts) of the Hermetic Order of the Golden Dawn. Dion Fortune elaborated on this concept in her book *Psychic Self-Defence*, published early in the twentieth century. Fortune describes defense against astral vampirism, astral entities that prey on the vital energy of their victims. Fortune also describes unintentional psychic vampires: people who unintentionally draw energy from others around them. Katherine Ramsland discussed this phenomenon in *Piercing the Darkness*. A few books, such as Konstantinos's *Vampires: The Occult Truth*, speak of intentional psychic vampires, people who consciously take energy from those around them. But these books were written about psychic vampires, not by them. It was only a matter of time before psychic vampires came forward to do so. A recent example of this is Michelle Belanger's excellent book *The Psychic Vampire Codex*.

Some individuals were recognized as vampiric as early as the nineteenth century. However, their vampirism was generally looked upon as an affliction. In recent years, those who have recognized their vampiric nature have created a spiritual path around this understanding. A vampire (also known as a Sanguinarian) is a person who lives a vampire lifestyle and has what they describe as a vampiric condition. Coming to a realization of one's vampire nature is referred to as "Awakening." Vampires believe that Awakening typically occurs during or shortly after puberty, though it can occur later. Symptoms of Awakening include: sensitivity to light (especially sunlight), affinity for darkness/night, switching sleeping patterns from nocturnal to diurnal, and thirst. Once awakened, vampires describe the following symptoms of their condition:

- A real need to consume the blood or life energy of others
- Heightened psychic abilities such as astral projection and powers of divination
- Sensitivity to light. This sensitivity does not prevent them from being in sunlight, though many report susceptibility to sunburn or sunstroke.
- Tendency toward a daytime sleep cycle
- Increased healing abilities
- Possible lengthened lifespan

Those committed to vampire spirituality replenish themselves by consuming the energy and/or blood of others in an ethical and consensual manner. Vampires of the Elorathian traditions (which have very seriously gone out of vogue in North America, as many people in the vampire community object strongly to being associated with Sebastian's approach to vampirism) refer to this process as *communion*. Someone from whom vampires get blood or life energy, whether voluntary or not, is referred to by vampires as a *source*. Someone who shares their blood or life energy with a vampire without obligation is known as a *donor*. Most donors are monogamous, offering themselves to only one vampire.

Sharing your energy with someone else is all very well and good if you consent to it. Having someone draw off your life energy without your knowledge and consent is another matter entirely. The individual drawing upon your energy may not be conscious of what they are doing. Such a person is referred to by vampires as an unawakened or latent vampire, someone who is naturally a vampire but whose vampiric tendencies have not yet fully manifested. Such people may never come to realize their vampire nature.

If someone with vampiric tendencies is intentionally drawing off your energy without your consent, then you need to take measures to sever the energetic ties with them and block them out. Again, most modern vampire traditions frown upon such activity in their membership. The code of conduct and etiquette of the Sanguinarium is the Black Veil, which was originally created in 1998 by Father Sebastian. Michelle Belanger undertook the task of revising this document for the general vampire in early 2000. The Black Veil is recognized by all of the various traditions of the vampire community. It encourages respect between differing vampire traditions and encourages sensibility and discretion in vampiric lifestyles. The latest version, updated by Belanger in 2002, has seven tenets:[58]

- *Discretion:* Respect yourself and present yourself so that others also respect you. Take care in revealing yourself. Explain what you are—not to shock, but to teach and to inform. Do not flaunt what you are, and know that whether you want them to or not, your actions will reflect upon the rest of the community. Share your nature only with those with the wisdom to understand and accept it, and learn to recognize these people.

58. Michelle Belanger, *The Psychic Vampire Codex* (York Beach, ME: Weiser, 2004), appendix III.

- *Diversity:* Among us, there are many different practices and many points of view. No single one of us has all the answers to who and what we are. Respect each person's individual choices and beliefs. Learn about them and share what you know. Our diversity is our strength, and we should not allow misunderstanding to weaken our community. Find the path that is right for you, and uphold this freedom for others.

- *Control:* Do not allow your darkness to consume you. You are more than just your hunger, and you can exercise conscious control. Do not be reckless. Always act with a mind toward safety. Never feed because you think this makes you powerful; feed because this is what you must do. Be true to your nature, but never use it as an excuse to endanger those around you.

- *Elders:* Give respect to those who have earned it. Anyone can claim a title, but a true leader will prove himself or herself through dedication, hard work, and great deeds. Even so, leaders should be guides and not dictators. Look to them as examples, but always decide for yourself what you must do. Respect the person, not the position, and understand that your choices are always your own.

- *Behavior:* Know that there are repercussions to every action, and that you alone are responsible for your decisions. Educate yourself about risky behaviors, then always act with wisdom and common sense. Do not allow others to abuse you, but also, do not selfishly abuse. Respect the rights of others and treat them as you would be treated.

- *Donors:* Feeding should occur between consenting adults. Allow donors to make an informed decision before they give of themselves to you. Do not take rapaciously from others, but seek to have an exchange that is pleasant and beneficial for all. Respect the life that you feed upon and do not abuse those who provide for you.

- **Community:** Reach out to others in your community. Exchange ideas, information, and support. Be hospitable to others, and appreciate hospitality when it is extended to you. Do not engage in illegal activity, for this can endanger us all. Seek to nurture our community and support all those who do the same.

Ghosts

EiGHT

Ghosts

Foul deeds will rise,
Though all the earth o'erwhelm them to men's eyes.

—Shakespeare, *Hamlet*

I don't want to go into lots of detail about hauntings and ghosts in this book. It is a subject that deserves a book of its own to do it justice. The only reason I am devoting a chapter to this subject is that one of the things that can be mistaken for a psychic attack is a haunting. The "attack" may actually be you perceiving a ghost in your vicinity.

The quantum concept of consciousness and/or information being stored in the potentiality of the unified field shows us the possibility that consciousness may exist separately from a living system. Multiple intersecting dimensions and/or parallel universes have been postulated in modern quantum mechanics. Since we are all "entangled"—that is, interconnected—one can easily see that there is a group consciousness at work in the world. Since everything that occurs is ultimately the result of one or more quantum mechanical events, the universe could be "inhabited" by an almost unlimited number of discrete, conscious entities. Since we can affect the world with our thoughts and with our will, we may actually create some of these entities. This explains many phenomena from Gods to spirits to fairies. Some appear to be localized, others nonlocalized. People seem to "resonate" with particular archetypes or God-forms. Some people are unable to detect them at all. I've heard some modern researchers refer to them as "resonance matrices." They can be very nonspecific, vague, and disperse in form, or very specific in appearance and mannerisms.

Thus it is easy to see that a person's consciousness could exist separately from one's body. Out-of-body experiences are one form of this. Ghosts are another.

Haunted locations are the result of one of two scenarios:

· A discarnate soul
· A "recording": this relies upon the principle of quantum encryption that I mentioned earlier.

The first situation, a discarnate soul, is commonly referred to as a ghost. Ghosts are generally believed to be the souls of people trapped between the physical and astral worlds through fear, guilt, anger, or desire. Ghosts may be encountered in houses where a person has died, especially if the deceased lived there a long time and/or their end was particularly traumatic. These discarnate people cannot hurt you, though their activities can be annoying or unsettling. When I attended Royal Roads Military College in Colwood, British Columbia, there was a ghost that wandered the halls of Hatley Castle (the headquarters building) at night, bumping and slamming doors. I understand that it is still there. One Wiccan of my acquaintance lived in a house where an elderly woman had died at about three in the morning. The ghost would turn the lights on in the bedroom at that time of the morning every few days. One of my colleagues at work has a ghost that keeps opening particular doors, even if they are secured.

Ghosts can only create serious problems if you feed them with fear. Even then this will only lead to you being distracted and clumsy, which in turn may set you up for an accident. In a situation like this you don't need to defend yourself. What you need to do is stay calm. Of course, if they don't bother you, you could just let them stay put and leave them alone. Hauntings are relatively rare.

The second situation is a far more likely cause and is not caused by a discarnate soul. It is a phenomena connected to psychometry. Sensitive people can detect the residue of unpleasant events that occurred in their surroundings. The structure that surrounds you or particular objects in your vicinity have "recorded" these unpleasant events. What is happening to you is what you might call "unwanted psychometry." You're picking up these influences unintentionally. It gives you "flashes" of images or impressions that can be startling and frightening. You can develop your psychometric skills to gain some control over this. Alternatively, you could clean the interior of the house, rearrange the furniture, and so on, to help clean out negative influences and improve the flow of chi. While doing this cleaning, you concentrate on putting emotions and ideas into your surroundings that are more beneficial. In effect you are endeavoring to "overwrite the program." Such measures take care of most situations perceived to be "hauntings."

A sensitive person might experience nightmares in environments full of negative energy. If you find someone "under attack" while they are asleep, *don't wake them*. It makes more sense for them to use the dream state that they are in. You should whisper encouragement into their ear as they sleep. Tell them they have the power to overcome this. Tell them that they have psychic weapons that they can use to defeat whatever is after them. Describe these weapons and encourage them to use them. Empower them. Of course, if it is you who suddenly realizes you are having such a nightmare, arm yourself in your imagination with whatever you need to deal with the situation. This is a similar situation to the defense of astral temples I described in chapter 5.

If you are dealing with a discarnate entity, you've got to do three things:

- Repair or bolster the victim's wards or aura to keep negative energy out. Sometimes these things draw energy out of the surroundings to manifest themselves, which explains the feelings of cold that are often experienced by people witnessing these situations. You need to stop this energy loss. These entities can't manifest if they can't get the energy to do so. No energy, no manifestation.
- Clear the negative energy out of the building or surroundings.
- Take action to, as Dion Fortune puts it, "break the contact."

I prefer Fortune's expression "break the contact," as it is a more accurate description of what is required. Breaking the contact is not the same as banishing; I discuss techniques for breaking contacts in chapter 11. Banishing is *not* a very useful technique to use in hauntings. For example, if a discarnate entity is bringing a lesson that you need, banishing will not "solve" this problem. The entity banished will be replaced with another bearing the same message. Examine the situation carefully first to determine if there is some message being relayed. Once the message is understood, the haunting may well take care of itself.

If this discarnate entity is trapped, you don't want to banish it. That's basically what has already happened. Establish communication. Find out what it is doing here. Establish this discarnate entity's understanding of its plight. This can be difficult at times. An entity not otherwise able to communicate might resort to knocking physical objects around to get attention. They get attention, all right, but not necessarily understanding. Some research into the history of the locale and the situation may be needed to shed light on the situation. Use of divinatory tools such as Tarot or crystals may help. Once you've established what the entity's need is, counsel it and give it what help you can to help set it free from its condition.

It is best to get a professional psychic to contact this discarnate spirit. Don't attempt it yourself if you don't have the expertise to handle the contact and to terminate it when you want to.

Nor do I recommend the use of Ouija boards to communicate with discarnate entities unless you know what you are doing. Ouija boards seem to be the most common tool used by people with no training to contact spirits. Teens often try out Ouija boards with unpleasant results. Either learn how to deal with these things or leave well enough alone.

A phenomenon often mistaken for a haunting is the poltergeist. Poltergeists are invariably the result of excess, uncontrolled emotions. Poltergeists are simply manifestations of extreme emotional energy. Usually the instigator is a teenager, not some ghost. The teen is sending that energy out there and it is causing those probabilities that Schrödinger described to collapse into reality in a big way, causing things to fall over, fly across the room, and so forth. The solution is to deal with the teenager's issues, not call in an exorcist. In cases of alleged poltergeists, look for a human epicenter. Again, no energy, no manifestation. In this case you are dealing with someone's unconscious will driving the situation. When you help the instigator deal with their angst and stress, the poltergeist ends.

Another phenomenon that resembles a haunting is what I'll refer to as "artificial elementals," or simulacrums. These are entities created out of the imagination and energy of the person sending negative energy at you. Artificial elementals or simulacrums are a thought-form projected at you by your attacker. They are a sort of nasty, disincarnate messenger. They can appear as a mist, a shape (human or otherwise), a ball of light, a shrouded figure, or even an image of the assailant. It is these simulacrums that probably gave rise to ancient legends of incubus and succubus.

Artificial elementals tend to be short-lived: their energy is limited and runs out rapidly, unless it is refreshed by their creator. Such nonphysical manifestations or simulacrums are often accompanied by astral lights. *Astral lights* is the traditional occult term used to describe the tiny silver sparks or motes of light that appear in and around an area where a manifestation of this type is occurring. The size and duration of astral lights are directly related to the strength of the manifestation causing them.

Focusing on a negative manifestation of any kind—such as the knocks and taps of minor poltergeist phenomena, or the antics of an artificial elemental—can facilitate a psychic connection that feeds and empowers it. There is an old adage: "If you take an interest in the supernatural, the supernatural takes an interest in you." Experiencing unexpected phenomena, peculiar sensations, or strange noises in the dead of night triggers an automatic response: you try to focus on the disturbance in order to identify and locate the source. Keep your guard up. Keep calm. Don't let panic set in. Focus first on identifying the source of the energy, using the techniques that I showed you earlier. Once you've identified the source, use the techniques in chapter 11 to block it or shut it down. No energy source, no manifestation.

Health

nine

Health

The scars of others should teach us caution.

—Saint Jerome

A key principle of psychic self-defense is "He who endures the longest usually wins." A corollary of this is "He who is healthiest endures longest." Psychic attacks cannot be maintained indefinitely, since they use vast amounts of energy and concentration. Victims lacking experience and knowledge must usually endure psychic attacks until the attacker runs out of steam—this will usually happen within a few days, a few weeks at most. Robert Bruce tells us that "weathering attacks also causes forced bio-energetic development; which in a way grows etheric callouses around one."[59] I'm not suggesting that you just sit back, suffer, and develop "etheric callouses," but you will suffer less if you are fit. Another consideration is that physical methods of defense use less energy than psychic ones. Thus it is best to make good use of physical methods whenever possible.

59. Robert Bruce, "White Light Shields," http://www.astraldynamics.com/tutorials/?BoardID=10&BulletinID=214 (accessed 22 October 2007).

Your ability to shield yourself is affected by such variable factors as daily stress, amount of sleep, the nature of the attack, your level of anxiety or confidence, and (if you are inexperienced) the number of distractions. As I mentioned earlier, the victim's vulnerabilities often dictate how a psychic attack proceeds and succeeds. Some of these vulnerabilities will be negative attitudes conditioned into you in childhood. Such weaknesses can be detected and exploited by sensitive and/or attentive enemies. Yet the most common vulnerabilities stem from the victim's poor health. A healthy body is hard to attack. Being physically weak makes you vulnerable.

I've written a lot in this book about eliminating energy blocks to enhance your ability to defend yourself magickally. There is an old Zen adage: "Ken-Zen Ichi Nyo" (Body and Mind Together). Magickal energy will flow through you best if your body is in good shape. One of the Warrior precepts that I listed in *Full Contact Magick* was: "Your body is your temple. Care for it!" If you want to be effective in psychic self-defense, you need to take this precept to heart.

In a defensive situation you need to be able to access and move energy rapidly. A healthy body is better able to channel defensive energy than an unhealthy one. A person who is in good shape has better reserves of energy and fewer energy blockages than someone who is unfit and infirm. Chi flows more efficiently through a body that is fit. Illness and fatigue can affect your mind's ability to function and focus. The better shape you are in, the more effective your magickal defenses will be.

I've already shown you some of the many techniques from Eastern forms of medicine and philosophy for manipulating chi. If you are having trouble accessing chi, I highly recommend using systems of exercise such as Chi Kung to improve both your health and the flow of energy through you.

Therefore, from a perspective of psychic self-defense, attending to your health and regularly exercising are important. Don't let yourself get overheated. Drink lots of fluids, get adequate rest, and eat properly. Don't let yourself become constipated. Also, take time every day for some quiet moments when you can center, internalize, manage personal energy, and eliminate stress.

What you eat has profound effects on your defensive readiness. It can affect your ability to raise or ground energy. The quality and quantity of food and exercise you get affects your energy and stamina. In turn, the quantity and quality of energy available to you affects the strength of your defenses. You're not going to be as effective in defense if you're hitting the wall because you missed a meal. Overeat and you'll inhibit your ability to raise energy. One of the reasons that the Wiccan ceremony of "cakes and wine" is included at the end of the ritual is that the consumption of food tends to ground us. If you're having trouble ridding yourself of surplus energy at the conclusion of a session of defensive magick, a simple meal can help to ground you. Overeating will ground you, too, perhaps at a time when grounding your energy is going to affect your magickal defense. Moderation is the best approach. A healthy diet will keep you in good shape to meet threats head-on at any time.

You should avoid sedatives, alcohol, and drugs. As I noted earlier, these can put you into states of mind that make it difficult for you to respond to psychic attack. Exhaustion and/or alcohol can quickly erode your ability to shield yourself. A high-fat, processed diet, or an excess of caffeine, tobacco, or alcohol, will affect your energetic levels and thought processes. A balanced, healthy diet will help to stabilize your energy and clarify your mind. This, in turn, will make your defensive magick more effective.

Fatigue and Light

I've heard arguments that light deters psychic attacks and/or that psychic attacks can't occur in daylight. This is ridiculous. Psychic attacks can occur at any time. Ideas such as this partially come out of the ancient ideas of negative magick being a "dark art." However, there is a basis for this belief that causes me to mention it in this chapter: psychic attacks do often occur at night. This isn't because light interferes with psychic attacks. It is because you are more vulnerable to such attacks when you are in certain states of mind, such as sleep states. You are also more vulnerable to psychic attack when you are fatigued.

Getting adequate rest is important if you want to maintain your energy levels. An old psychic self-defense technique suggests that when a psychic attack is under way, you should try to remain in a waking state of consciousness. The idea is that you are better able to defend yourself if you are in a conscious state. The problem with this idea is that if you remain in waking consciousness too long, avoiding needed sleep, you will ultimately render yourself incapable of defending yourself due to fatigue and the resulting inability to focus. Lack of sleep can ultimately lead to paranoia and hallucinations.

If someone is launching psychic attacks against you while you sleep, a better alternative may be to change your sleep pattern. Your assailant may be counting on you sleeping at night in order to take advantage of your sleep states to make you vulnerable. Changing your normal hours of sleep for a while will make it more likely that you'll be in waking consciousness when the attack comes. Once you identify and neutralize the attack, you can return to your regular sleep schedule, secure in the knowledge that you've foiled the assailant.

Another measure that helps is moving your bed to a new position. This is a feng shui trick that alters the flow of chi in the room. It won't stop the attack, but it may minimize the effects while you come up with a strategy to deal with it.

Another important tool for maintaining your ability to defend yourself is grounding. This is such an important subject that the next chapter will be entirely devoted to it.

Grounding

ten

Grounding

When we are harmed by others,
we are usually not grounded in our foundations.

—Christopher Penczak, *The Witch's Shield*

Grounding is simply creating an outlet to drain off excess or negative energy within you. Psychic Craig Hamilton-Parker states: "Learning to close down after doing your psychic work is even more important than opening up in the first place. When I'm not working psychically I keep my centers firmly shut. If I tuned in to every vibration that came my way I'd soon be a gibbering wreck. Psychics that push their clairvoyance on you at every opportunity are normally not much good; they waste their energy."[60]

Working with energy in defensive magick can sometimes cause a surplus of energy to build up inside you. Sometimes this is because tension or blocks in one of your chakras is impeding the flow of energy. If you are doing magick the way you're supposed to, you'll let energy flow through you, acting

---

60. Craig Hamilton-Parker, "Psychic Self-Defence," http://www.psychics
.co.uk/aura/aura_protect.html (accessed 12 October 2007).

as a channel or conductor of the energy without impeding it or storing up surplus energy. However, even experienced magickal practitioners can have "off" days when they don't feel 100 percent. Even an experienced person can have this surplus buildup of energy occur. If you find yourself feeling restless, confused, distracted, lightheaded, dizzy, or unfocused following magickal work, this is an indication that you have such a buildup and need to ground it out. There are several things that you can do to alleviate the problem. You should always ground yourself after doing magick. Actually, even if you haven't been doing energy work, it is a good idea to clean out your energy systems and ground on a regular basis. Norse counselor Ormungandr puts it this way: "We all like to take a physical shower, but how often do we 'cleanse' our mind and emotions?"[61]

There are three basic steps in this grounding process:

- First, drain excess/negative energy into the earth. The earth forms a better "energy sink" than the atmosphere. It conducts the energy away from you more efficiently. You are not harming the earth by directing this energy into it. The earth breaks it down like it breaks down organic matter to return it in a usable form.

- Next, incorporate a "closing ritual" that signals to your subconscious that you've shut down the open channels. This can be as simple as using a closing gesture such as stamping your foot, clapping your hands, placing your hands on the ground, or moving your strong arm in a downward motion across your body.

- Finally, eat a light meal. Food is grounding. As I pointed out earlier, consuming food and beverages grounds out energy and returns a person to normal waking conscious-

61. Ormungandr, "Spirit of Yggdrasil" (accessed 18 October 2006).

ness. One way to help keep your psychic centers closed is by keeping your stomach full. Pagan author Patricia Telesco tells us that "meat has the capacity to deconstruct static, and root vegetables represent that 'grounding' force for which we seek. The crunchy sound (in raw form) also seems to help."[62]

Don't use alcohol to ground energy. Alcohol is a drug (a depressant) that alters the mind. It does ground the energy, but it also leaves you open to negative energy, as I pointed out earlier. Drink enough of it, and you'll become an energy sink, drawing energy out of those around you. I've seen people attend rituals drunk and completely flatten any attempts by others in the Circle to raise any sort of energy. It all gets sucked out of the Circle into the drunk. If you feel the need to use some sort of soporific to slow yourself down, try valerian tea.

A quick way to ground out surplus energy is simply to place your hands on the ground and let it flow out of your hands into the earth. An alternative is to imagine that you are putting down roots through your feet and let the surplus pass into the earth through your feet as you stand. In defensive situations I imagine myself digging in, anchoring myself and letting the energy run out through that anchor. In either case, imagine the surplus energy returning to the earth from which it came. One of my favorite grounding techniques is going out and working in the garden. I find that touching the soil naturally grounds out my surplus energy and restores my balance.

Grounding is also a useful way to handle overwhelming emotions like excessive anger that may arise from psychic attacks. Anger is a natural reaction to psychic attack, but it

---

62. Patricia Telesco, "Psychic Self Defense For Festivals (and Beyond)," (28 August 2002), www.witchvox.com/va/dt_va.html?a=usny&c=festtips&id=4661 (accessed 15 October 2007).

can cloud your judgment and hence your ability to effectively defend yourself. You cannot let anger get control of you in a fight. Grounding is a useful technique for controlling such emotions.

Sometimes you will be called upon to help ground one of your colleagues. It is best to make sure that you have centered and grounded yourself before you attempt this. You may also want to use a warding technique such as shielding to set up a protective screen around you and the person you are grounding to prevent any further exterior energy from making a bad situation worse (I'll speak of these techniques in the next chapter). Cutting this person off from the flow of surplus energy around them is a very important step: if you don't do this before grounding them, the energy will be pouring into them as fast as you draw it out.

Ground the person by talking them through the procedure. Let the excess energy pass into the earth through their feet. You may have them ground by holding a staff and using it as a sort of lightning rod to let the excess chi ground into the earth. Having the person hold a stone with grounding properties such as hematite may also be useful. If you are experienced in the use of chi, you can use yourself as a lightning rod to ground another person. Don't try this unless you are competent at grounding yourself. If the person you are grounding has no magickal training, teach them how to set up a simple ward for themselves before you leave them. After performing grounding for another, it is a good idea to ground and center yourself.

In *Full Contact Magick* I described a means of grounding called Putting Down Roots. In a defensive context you can modify this to the technique I call Digging In. Start in Entering Tranquility posture, then bring your feet together, hands at your sides. Imagine yourself being anchored to the ground beneath you. You are anchored to the earth, part of the earth beneath you. You become one with it. Sweep your hands up in an arc to either side of you until they are over your head, your palms facing each other. Bring the palms down, still parallel to one another, along the front of your body, and then bring your hands back to your sides. Do this three times.

As you do this the first time, breathe in as you bring your hands up over your head. Then as you exhale, imagine the energy running down the front of your body into the ground, which is part of you. As you do this a second time, breathe in again and exhale while imagining the energy running down your back into the ground. For the third and final repetition, breathe in one more time and then exhale while imagining the energy running down the center of your body into the ground. To finish, draw back both hands to your sides, make a fist with your hands briefly in a sealing gesture, and then return your hands to your sides, palms facing to the front.

Another Chi Kung exercise that you'll find useful in clearing out stagnant or negative energy buildups is what I call Swinging Arms. In this exercise, start in the Entering Tranquility posture. Raise your arms to the side to shoulder height. Then let them fall, one passing in front of you and the other behind, turning in the direction of the arm in front. Swing back to the front with arms raised to each side and then twist the other way, letting the other arm go in front this time. Repeat the motion, twisting from side to side, arms swinging across your body. As the arms come up to your sides, breathe in and imagine yourself filling with positive energy. As your arms swing across your body to either side, breathe out and imagine the negative energy streaming out of your fingers away from your body. You can imagine this as tossing balls of dark energy with your hands each time they swing across your body.

Another useful grounding exercise can be used while walking. Imagine that the foot on your strong side sends energy out and that the foot on your weak side draws energy in. Every time your strong foot touches the ground, imagine negative energy being grounded out of you. Every time your weak foot touches the ground, imagine positive energy coming in. A variation on this is a tapping exercise that you can do with a staff or walking stick. Every time the stick touches the ground, energy is transferred. Odd numbered taps (first, third, and so on) send negative energy into the ground, and even taps (second, fourth, and so on) draw positive energy up. This is a technique that many Pagan security groups such as the Guardians use in securing ritual areas. You'll note that it is a variation on the idea of receptive and projective hands that I described earlier.

Patricia Telesco suggests the following method for grounding: "I sit down and hold my hands out, palm upward, gathering those vibrations into my hands *only*. Do not accept it into yourself. Next, I put my hands on the ground and let Mother [Earth] accept the vibrations (she handles dirt very well)."[63]

Another common grounding technique involves closing down the chakras, one after the other. Start with the "brow center." Visualize the light there dimming. You can even imagine closing an iron door over it. Repeat this procedure for the throat center, heart center, solar plexus, spleen center, and base center. Then imagine light cascading out of your crown center to give yourself a "psychic shower" to wash away any remaining stress. Next, imagine yourself filling with light from your crown center. Finally, visualize the light at your crown center fading. Imagine closing an iron door over the crown center too, if you choose. Check all of your chakras to make sure they are shut down.

---

63. Patricia Telesco, "Psychic Self Defense For Festivals (and Beyond)."

Another visualization technique that can help you ground can be done when you are soaking in the bathtub. Many people like to create a purification bath by adding pinches of sea salt and/or herbs. If adding salts and herbs to the water puts you in the right frame of mind, go for it. Lie comfortably in the bath. As you soak, imagine all of your stress and negativity being drawn from you into the water. Immerse yourself for a moment from the top of your head to your toes. When you pull the plug to run out the water, imagine that the water is carrying away all of your negative energy with it.

Another common grounding and purification technique is smudging, which is basically immersing yourself in fragrant smoke of incense or herbs. Let the smoke billow all over you. Imagine the smoke carrying away negative energy. Physically step over the incense burner several times, back and forth as you focus on cleansing your aura with the incense. Imagine the smoke carrying away the negative energy. Some like to follow this up by running a lighted white candle over their aura, focusing on weak spots to "cauterize" and seal them.

One energy absorption technique that I've seen involves imagining a shiny jet-black ball about the size of a tennis ball floating before you in the center of the room. You imagine this ball spinning counterclockwise. As it spins you see it attracting black negative energy from the surrounding area. Imagine black strings, sparks, or clots of negative energy being drawn from the walls, ceiling, floor, and furniture. You can direct this spinning black ball slowly around the room as it gathers up all the negative energy. As it fills up with negative energy it steadily grows in size.

Once you consider the ball to be large enough, imagine the spin reversing, the ball now spinning clockwise. The instant that you reverse the spin you also imagine the ball changing in color to brilliant white. Once you've established this, let the white ball expand out and be absorbed back into your dwelling. The energy has been converted and is now harmless. This is an example of transforming the vibration or resonance of the energy involved.

Now that you've learned how to ground yourself, it's time to show you how to use, in practical psychic defense techniques, all of the principles of magick and quantum theory that I've told you about. This is what we'll do in the next chapter.

Warding Techniques

Warding Techniques

God grants liberty only to those who love it,
and are always ready to guard and defend it.

—Daniel Webster, June 3, 1834

A s I mentioned earlier in this book, some people take the approach summed up in the old adage that the "best defense is a good offense" when dealing with psychic self-defense. There's a lot of truth to this adage, but I'd like to point out again that Sun Tzu once said that the general who wins without fighting is the better general. I don't want you to fight your assailant; I want you to neutralize him. I want you to learn how to use the assailant's own energy to defeat him.

Remember, you aren't the only one who needs to be concerned about defense. It is an issue for your assailant, too: weaknesses in his defenses are an issue you can take advantage of. Generally, those who project telepathic malice at anyone else are lowering their own defenses. While they are focusing their will on the attack, their defenses are neglected. This allows the victim of their attack to get in underneath the assailant's wards to neutralize the malice. Understanding the defense techniques that follow will not only allow you to enhance your defenses, it will also give you a better understanding of how to exploit your assailant's defenses.

Many of the old magickal techniques for psychic self-defense involve binding your assailant in some way. I do not recommend binding techniques. Any sort of magick designed to "bind" or otherwise hinder the person sending negative energy at you will invariably establish a link to that person. This you absolutely do not want. Remember the old magickal adage: "Whatever you bind you're bound to." Remember that what you are trying to do is divert or ground out this negative energy. Binding techniques just make this harder, if not impossible. Binding techniques will make it easier for your assailant to connect to you. Binding is more of that "power over" stuff that I described earlier. You don't need to dominate the assailant. You just need to control your situation.

To affect you, a psychic attack must access your subconscious mind using the entanglements that connect us through the unified field. From your subconscious the attack can access your conscious reality and physical body. As I noted earlier, the negative energy coming in will cause you to start resonating with it, bringing on negative symptoms as you begin to entrain with it. Obsessing about a threatening situation just helps establish this contact. There are various things that you can do to help you break concentration on these threats and help you distance your thoughts from them and focus on your defense.

Hex Breakers
Sometimes what you need is a technique to break off the negative contact in order to give yourself space to react to the attack. Believe it or not, one of the best "hex breakers" is laughter. Laughing at the assailant and their attempts to cause problems

for you is a good way to minimize your anxieties. I'm not saying that laughter should be your only defense: I'm just saying that laughter can help you get into the right state of mind to conduct your defense effectively. Of course you have to be pretty confident to laugh at an attack in progress; most people would find this rather hard to do in difficult situations. So let's look at some easier methods.

Maybe you've become uncomfortable because someone is staring at you? Perhaps this is because the person staring at you is directing negative energy at you (intentionally or not). Don't look them in the eyes. Doing so just enhances the link. Instead, look at their "third eye," the area above and between their eyes. Avoiding eye contact is a very old method in many different cultures that can be used to resist the influence of someone trying to dominate or intimidate you. Avoiding eye contact effectively derails one of the main routes into your subconscious mind. Remember me telling you earlier about energy following intent? Intent is typically directed along one's line of sight. Breaking this contact gives you time to activate shields, using techniques I'll describe later in this chapter.

Another common entry point for negative energy is the chakra in the area of your solar plexus. As I mentioned earlier, in Asian medicine and martial arts this area just behind and about three inches below the navel is an energy storage area known as the Dantian. To protect this area of your body, you need to move into a modified version of the Entering Tranquility posture that I described earlier. Starting from Entering Tranquility, we can move into a posture that blocks out outside energy. I'm simply expanding upon a very old, reliable defense technique here.

Stand as I told you to in Entering Tranquility, but modify the posture by drawing your feet together so they are touching:

Placing the feet together seals off the lower part of you body's aura. Next, draw your strong arm down across your body in a chopping motion to help you visualize breaking the negative contact with your solar plexus area. Then interlace your fingers, laying your hands over your solar plexus, elbows pressed to your sides. Doing this will effectively block off all outside access to your body's energy channels.

Of course you can't just stand there indefinitely: this maneuver is meant to seal your "circuits" from psychic attack, giving you a respite during which you can gather your resources, recharge yourself, and select an appropriate defensive response. This technique is often referred to in older texts as "closing the auric circuit," as this posture closes several of the main etheric circuits in the body, preventing entrance of external forces. This posture links the chakras in your hands with the solar plexus chakra, or Dantian.

A similar technique involves two assistants hugging the person to be protected. These two (or more) people simply surround the victim, put up their shields, and hug the victim. This "group hug" surrounds the victim with the wards or shields of others. It can also be used as a short-term solution, to get the victim grounded to start building up their own defenses.

Creating Inattention

There is a useful technique that can be used in situations where you wish to go unnoticed that I call Creating Inattention. This technique resembles the mirroring techniques that I will describe in the next chapter, but unlike mirroring techniques, which I don't care for, this inattention technique is quite useful. Like the hex breakers, this isn't intended to be a permanent defense. It is only a technique designed to give you breathing space to create a more effective defense.

This inattention or "invisibility" technique takes advantage of people's natural tendency to be inobservant. Inattention is more prevalent than you might imagine. Daniel Simons of the University of Illinois and Christopher Chabris of Harvard University conducted a famous experiment in inattention.[64] In their study, participants in the experiment were asked to watch a video in which two groups of people wearing black and white T-shirts pass a basketball back and forth among themselves. The participants were subjected to an attention-focusing device; for example, they were told to count how many times the basketball is passed between the people in the white shirts. In the midst of this video clip, either a woman holding an open umbrella or a man dressed in a gorilla suit strolls through the middle of the game and passes out of sight.

Simons and Chabris found that, on average, *50 percent of the experiment participants didn't see the gorilla or the woman with the umbrella*. I mentioned earlier that we only pay attention to about two thousand of the four billion of bits of information that we take in during waking consciousness. This experiment is proof of that. You can check out these videos for yourself at the University of Illinois Visual Cognition Lab website.[65]

Visualize yourself completely surrounded by a camouflage surface, clad in a sort of camouflage surface that completely covers you, or surrounded by a surface that gradually takes on the pattern of your surroundings like a chameleon. I prefer the chameleon visualization myself. Focus on this visualization for a few minutes and imagine it becoming self-sustaining. This

---

64. Ormungandr, "Spirit of Yggdrasil," Daniel Simons and Christopher Chabris, "Gorillas in Our Midst: Sustained Inattentional Blindness For Dynamic Events," *Perception*, vol. 28 (20 June 1999), 1059–1074.

65. Daniel J. Simons, Visual Cognition Lab, University of Illinois, http:// viscog.beckman.uiuc.edu/djs_lab/demos.html (accessed 22 October 2007).

technique won't make you invisible. Those in your vicinity can still see you. What it will do is to help manipulate or desensitize the attention of those around you. You use your will to affect the variables in this situation to create this reality. They see you, but they tend not to notice you. More importantly, if someone is reaching out psychically trying to locate you, this inattention technique makes it harder for them to do so.

Wards

Many of the techniques of psychic self-defense involve putting up what are commonly referred to as wards or "shields." A ward is an active psychokinetic shield. When energy is thrown at you, a ward will divert this energy, making it veer away from you. Patricia Telesco tells us that "having your shield in place decreases the chance of picking up someone else's stress considerably."[66] Unless you want to be intimate with people around you, it is probably a good idea to keep your wards up.

One of the things that I like about wards or shields, especially from the standpoint of inexperienced people, is that they are a unidirectional defensive technique. All of the warding techniques that follow involve creating an energetic "bubble." This energy bubble forms the framework for the ward that we use to protect ourselves or a location from all directions. Even if you aren't very good yet at identifying from where negative energy is coming at you, you can protect yourself with these techniques.

How does a sphere of energy protect us? Obviously if you create a protective sphere such as a magick Circle, you can still walk through it (although doing so may disrupt the energy unless you do this properly). If you can walk through it, how does it stop the incoming energy? Many of the old texts describe defenses made up of the correct vibrations or light of a certain

---

66. Patricia Telesco, "Psychic Self Defense For Festivals (and Beyond)."

color, and this is a clue to the process. This protective energy sphere has a particular resonance. When the negative energy with a different vibration comes at you, it can't get in because when it touches this sphere it is disrupted. The interference caused as it reaches the protective sphere causes it to change frequency as it entrains with the frequency of the sphere. This is that principle of entrainment that I discussed earlier in this book. In effect, your protective sphere filters out all frequencies other than its resonance.

There's another way to look at this. Remember Schrödinger's wave equation? Schrödinger told us that reality is the result of interactions of waves of probabilities of different outcomes. Think of your protective sphere as a wave surface that you create to intersect with the waves of probability that your assailant sends at you. Thus the surface of this sphere is a place where these waves interact to create a reality that you control.

Here are some techniques using energy bubbles:

Shielding

The type of ward that I normally recommend to beginners is a technique I call shielding. Many writers refer to a person's energy field as their aura. This energy field can be made into your ward or shield, and it becomes your first line of defense. This is my own preference, as this "mobile" ward goes everywhere I go. Another option is to create a ward that is anchored to a physical location. You set the ward up and link it to the earth energy in that place. Typically, when setting up a static ward such as this, it is associated with or "anchored" to a physical object or building. I will return to fixed wards in a moment. Let's look first at "mobile" wards.

You can create this spherical personal ward by using the Holding the Ball exercise I discussed in *Full Contact Magick*. You can also use the Pushing the Sky exercise that I taught you earlier in this book. If you are a novice, it may assist you at first to trace out the perimeter of the ward on the ground around you. Doing so will help you visualize how far to let the energy ball expand.

Stand in the Entering Tranquility posture. Position your hands to start Pushing the Sky. Pause and draw on the universal energy. Swing your arms upward, breathing in and drawing in energy. Pause with your hands over your head and build up the energy while holding your breath for a few seconds. Then push upward, releasing the energy. Imagine it cascading down around you like a fountain of water, forming a spherical ward around you as it does so. Once you have released the energy, let your arms fall in an arc to your sides, hands now relaxed and hanging normally. As you are doing this, you are focusing your will on this ward, causing the quantum potentiality to manifest this energetic sphere. Thus you are using your imagination to define the ward and your will to create it.

If you have set up a spherical ward like this properly, you will notice that the temperature inside the ward seems to increase slightly. If you are a beginner, it is useful to use the receptive ability of your hands that I noted earlier to test the boundaries of your ward. Doing so will confirm that you've made the ward the size that you expected. It will also give you an idea as to how strong it is. If it feels weak to you, you can always put more energy into it. If this is the case, check that you've eliminated any energy blocks in your body and send more energy into the ward, letting the chi run through you freely. Exploring the boundaries with your hands also will give you an idea as to the feel or resonance of your ward. If it doesn't feel quite right, take it down and start again. You should feel that same heat or tingling that you noticed when the chi was flowing in the exercises that I described in the chapter on using energy.

To close the ward down, stand in the middle with your arms spread wide. Release the focus of your will, causing the energy to return to the unified field of quantum potentiality. Imagine the energy sphere collapsing in on itself. Gather the energy in, encircling it with your arms as if bringing it into the position in front of your chest once more. Absorb it into the Dantian energy center in your abdomen (behind and below the navel), pressing your hands over this area for a moment. Let the surplus energy run out into the earth beneath you. Then take a moment to stand in Entering Tranquility. Breathe deeply a few times, letting the chi within you come back into balance. When you take your shield down for any reason, prepare yourself for a sudden inrushing of energy. Be prepared to ground out the surplus so that it doesn't build up inside of you and make you ill.

There are any number of ways to imagine this spherical ward when you are creating it. When creating your ward it may help if you imagine the surface of your shield as a sort of grid or cage that captures the incoming negative energy and grounds it into the earth where it touches the earth under your feet. Alternatively, you can visualize being surrounded by a "net" or a sphere of energy. This technique simply takes the energy directed at you and places it back in the universal pool. Another way of thinking of this form of defense is as a filter that protects you from unwanted energy. Your will selects what passes through the shield, because your will is setting the resonance of the sphere that surrounds you.

When you create this ward, imagine it to be capable of diverting incoming energy from all directions at once. Some authors recommend creating two layers: a tight core around your body and a secondary level about ten feet from your body.

This secondary shield is intended to redirect objects before they can reach the inner core shield. I don't find this necessary myself, but if it makes you more comfortable to do it this way, go right ahead. Actually, you needn't create a very large personal ward. It can be just outside of the surface of your skin. Once you get good at this, creating a ward like this becomes an unconscious process; you can create and sustain the field without consciously thinking about it. As your shield becomes self-sustaining and self-propagating, it will become much stronger.

One simple form of this technique, sometimes called the Tower of Light[67] technique, requires you to visualize this sphere as glowing with intense, bright blue light or white light, like a magnesium flare surrounding your body. This visualization will assist you in achieving the correct resonance within the ward. Focus your will on this spherical ward to "program" it in order to filter out unwanted energy. Just as you do with the other shielding techniques that I'm showing you, make the sphere vibrate with a particular frequency that will not allow the wrong frequencies in.

It often helps to visualize the energy of this net or sphere "thickening" or "hardening" around you. If it helps, you can imagine this shield as a fortress. I've heard this shielding technique referred to as an "iron wall" or "stone tower" visualization. One way of imagining this is to see yourself building a brick wall around yourself with each brick glowing blue, knowing that you are safe inside this wall. Remember to seal such a space above and below, as you don't want anything getting under or over the "wall." Another variation of this method is to imagine yourself protected by plate glass. It is important to imagine the negative energy being diverted by your shield and

---

67. "Psychic Self-Defense: Tower of Light," A Witch's Cauldron, http://www
.pathcom.com/~newmoon/defence.htm (accessed 22 October 2007).

flowing into the earth. Imagine the shield as a selective, one-way filter. Your energy can pass out, but unwanted energy cannot pass in.

These shielding techniques take advantage of the principles of karma. You'll notice that they are designed not to reflect anything back to the source. Your assailant will not see anything happening to you and will get the impression that their efforts are having no effect, which will hopefully be disheartening for them. At the same time, they are setting themselves up to get back the karmic consequences of acting in this antisocial manner. You will be doing nothing negative or destructive, which leaves you with no karmic debt.

Practice these shielding techniques over and over. Get the feel of the energy flowing through you and around you. Feel your shields locking into place. Memorize this feeling so that when you need to use it later, it will be easier to visualize and activate on command.

Stationary Wards and Circles

In some instances you may want to put up a ward to protect a specific location, such as your residence or a ritual site. The linking of a protective shield to a certain location is the basis of the many ancient systems of magick that utilize the magick Circle as a means of defense. Circles are used extensively in ceremonial magick and Wicca. I don't intend to describe the various rituals from the many different magickal traditions involving Circle casting here. I want to focus here on the idea of a Circle as a defense only. Elaborate ritual is not necessary for this; it is possible to put up a Circle without any ceremony involved.

You can create this stationary ward by using the same Holding the Ball exercise or the Pushing the Sky technique that I showed you earlier. It is no different than creating a personal ward. It may be easier for you at first if you trace out the perimeter of the ward on the ground around the area that you wish to enclose. Doing so will help you visualize how far to let the energy ball expand.

Stand in the Entering Tranquility posture in the center of the area that you want to enclose with the ward. Position your hands to start Pushing the Sky. Pause and find that energy out there that you want to draw on. Swing your arms upward, breathing in and drawing this energy in. Pause with your hands over your head and let the energy build up pressure inside you while you hold your breath for a few seconds. Then push upward, releasing the energy. See it in your mind cascading down around you, forming a spherical ward around you as it does so. Once you have released the energy, let your arms fall in an arc to your sides. As you are doing this, you are focusing your will on this ward, causing the quantum potentiality to manifest this energetic sphere. Thus you are using your imagination to define the ward and your will to create it.

As you are doing this, you are focusing your will on this ward, causing the quantum potentiality to manifest this energetic sphere. Imagine it enclosing and protecting the area. Use any of the visualizations that I described for creating a personal ward to enhance your creation of this shield.

Circle casting in traditions of Wicca and ceremonial magick is simply a ritual variation of this process. A ritual/defensive Circle is not really a Circle. It is a sphere of energy, just like the personal spherical ward that I was describing earlier. The Circle is simply where this sphere intersects the surface on which it is set up. If you normally create a magickal Circle with ritual, and this makes you comfortable, then by all means do it that way. Just bear in mind that if you have to, you don't need a ritual performance to create a defensive Circle. You can put a defensive Circle up in an instant if you need to.

If it helps you to walk around the perimeter of the Circle with either a ritual dagger (such as the Wiccan athame), a ritual sword, or a wand to help visualize creating impregnable boundaries and cutting yourself off from the mundane world, then go ahead and do it. Just remember that once you master visualization, you'll be able to create it in your mind without having to use any Magickal Weapons at all. In an emergency you can just switch a Circle on around you with a thought. I prefer to use my Holding the Ball technique to create the spherical shield that is the Circle, but if you have another technique that helps you to visualize this process and it works for you, then go ahead and use it. This is all about using what works for you.

Again, I'm not going to go into any specific ritual detail here. I describe the standard Wiccan Circle casting procedure in my book *Full Contact Magick*. Don't get hung up on the ritual detail; I encourage you to use whatever words come from the heart to make the necessary elemental connections. The energy flows much easier when one is relaxed, and you're more likely to be relaxed if you are working with something familiar to you. If you are standing all tensed up in the quarters of your Circle desperately trying to remember your lines for invoking the Guardians, you are going to tense up.

As I noted earlier, tensing up will impede the flow of energy. In a defensive Circle you absolutely don't want that. You want a free-flowing connection to energy. Reading the words off of a card or out of a book isn't much better; if you do that, you are focusing on the paper instead of reaching out to connect with the elemental energy. Use whatever words you wish to make this connection. It is better not to use any words at all than to stumble about trying to remember set lines.

The principal difference between a personal ward and a fixed one like a ritual Circle is that with a fixed shield you occasionally find that you have to leave (and probably later return to) the area bounded by this fixed sphere of energy. As I mentioned earlier, this spherical ward that you have created, whether a personal ward or a Circle, is neither solid nor impermeable. It is a filter meant to keep energy out, not solid objects. Household pets and people can walk through this spherical ward at will, briefly disrupting the ward's energy. This may momentarily cause some discomfort for the people within the ward, but it shouldn't cause any serious problems unless the ward is extremely weak.

Various ritual methods have been devised over the years to allow people to walk in and out of magickal Circles. The most common technique for creating a portal in a ritual Circle, through which one can pass without upsetting the balance of the rest of the Circle, is commonly called "cutting a doorway." The magician, using their hand or the Magickal Weapon that they used to cast the Circle, outlines an archway at the perimeter of the Circle. As the magician does so, they imagine that the energy draws back around it so that it creates a portal.

If this technique or something similar works for you, then go ahead and use it. You'll find it easier working with the familiar in stressful situations. Remember that as you create this portal you should focus your will onto it to make the quantum potentiality coalesce into this portal. If you used a Magickal Weapon to assist you in doing this, lay it on the ground across the threshold and step out of the Circle. When you re-enter, pick up the Magickal Weapon and retrace the archway in reverse. Imagine the portal closing in on itself and sealing once again. Let the portal collapse back into the unified field of infinite probabilities once more. The only problem with this technique is that while the portal is open, anything and everything can pass through it. This defeats the purpose of the ward.

A method that I prefer is what I call "slipping through." Instead of "cutting a doorway," allow yourself to shift into resonance with the energetic ward sphere briefly and slip through the matrix without disturbing it. To re-enter the Circle you simply do this in reverse. Stand next to the part of the Circle that you want to leave or enter through. Put yourself in Entering Tranquility posture. Reach out with your mind and sense the energy of the Circle that you've created. You may find this easier if you reach out with your hands until you encounter the perimeter of the energy sphere that is the Circle. Let the vibrations of the energy of the Circle entrain with your own. Remember the toning exercises that I told you about in chapter 6? Just as you can feel when everyone in the group "clicks" together in one frequency, you will feel yourself and the Circle energy "click." As soon as you sense that entrainment, just step through to the outside of the Circle. You simply repeat this process to get back in. This doesn't disrupt the energy of the Circle, and it doesn't create an opening to let negative energies in.

Don't let fearful people, mentally or emotionally unbalanced people, or intensely negative people work with you in Circle. Their energy can disrupt the defenses that you are trying so hard to erect. There you are, trying to block out negative influences with your ward, and the interior is filled with negative influences from the people that you brought in with you! If you have to bring such people into the Circle to, for example, protect them, then be sure to monitor the energy around you carefully. Have some emotionally stable and energetically strong people in there with you to help keep the energies in balance.

Push-Pull

It isn't necessary to put up a shield to protect yourself from negative energy. Once you've become good at identifying the flow of the negative energy, you can work directly on that flow to redirect it or shut it off.

A very effective defensive maneuver that you can use if you are good at detecting and moving energy is something that I call "The Pull." This measure stems from an ancient martial arts adage: "if they push, you pull; if they pull, you push." You use them against themselves. So your assailant wants to stream negative energy at you? All right. Relax. Surround yourself with a feeling of peace and security. This will help you to deal with any negative stuff streaming by in what happens next. You don't want to "entrain" with the negative energy that you'll be handling.

Now, reach out with your mind and find out where the stream is coming from. Got it? OK. Now open up your channels, "grab" this stream, and mentally pull. Hard. Let the negative energy discharge into the earth, grounding it, returning it to the unified field whence it came. The assailant on the other end, pushing that energy for all they're worth, suddenly winds up flat on their face, drained completely. Do this correctly, and I guarantee your assailant is not going to want to try that again on you. They're not going to be able to stop it until you've already drained them.

I find that this "pull" absorption technique is excellent, but remember that it depends on the state of consciousness of the user. You need to maintain control of your own energy and emotions as you use this technique. You especially don't want to be angry when you use this technique. If you are, that may simply connect you with the anger that is being directed at you. You don't want to entrain with the negative energy you are handling. Maintain a sense of serenity to distance yourself from this negative energy.

If the assailant becomes aware that you've erected a defensive ward or shield, they may attempt to defeat this measure by draining energy out of it. Alternatively, they may attempt to wear you down by trying to draw energy away from you while you are vulnerable, your shields down, such as when you are trying to sleep. If you've been working with the energy techniques that I described earlier, you should be able to sense this "pull" on your energy. This is where practice in wielding energy is so important—it helps you to establish the direction of the energy flow around you and lets you redirect it at will.

One way to set a trap for such an attempt is to first surround yourself with a shield or protective energy bubble. Fill this space with the feeling of relaxed calm and friendliness. Focus on this feeling for between ten to fifteen minutes, using your imagination to make it self-sustaining. Imagine the field continuing to function at full strength at all times. The idea is that if the assailant latches on to this and draws at the energy, they find they are filled with feelings that neutralize their anger and frustration. This is a good technique to use while you are resting or sleeping, since it is more or less "automatic."

A field or shield set up around a location in this fashion typically lasts about a week. Alternatively, you could charge this energy field with feelings of confusion or the inability to concentrate. Imagine the person attacking you being unable to concentrate or focus. This technique is not as effective as the shielding techniques described earlier. A befuddled enemy can still hurt you. If they don't realize that their negative energy is impacting you, then this feeling won't be that effective. You also run the risk of it affecting you to make you befuddled yourself. You may have to put a little extra time and care into building this sort of ward should you decide to use it.

A much more effective measure to deal with people trying to suck energy away from you stems from that same "if they push, you pull; if they pull, you push" principle. So they want to latch on to your energy and pull? OK. Relax. Surround yourself with a feeling of peace and security. Open your energy channels. Then let them have the full charge. Don't give them *your* energy. Instead, think of yourself as a floodgate that is opening to let the full power of the universe flow through you. Let the energy of the universe race out of the unified field through you at them. Here they are pulling for all they're worth and suddenly they get hit by an energy tsunami that fries their circuits.

I call this technique "The Push." Neutralize their attack by identifying the emotions that are motivating them (e.g., hate) and imaging the opposite (such as love). Once the opposite is fully fixed in your mind, send it off and watch this ground out the attack. This is an excellent technique if you can do it, as it absolutely snuffs out such attacks. At the successful conclusion of this technique, you should feel ecstatic and energetic.

Cutting Links
Earlier I described simple techniques to cut energetic links to give you time to respond defensively. I also discussed phenomena such as simulacrums that an assailant can send at you to cause you problems and distress. Let's look at some more involved and detailed techniques for severing energetic links in order to deal with such situations.

If you detect someone's energetic ties linked to you, there are various ways to detach them. Dion Fortune's ritual of severance in her classic book *Psychic Self-Defence* is an example of this. As I mentioned in the earlier chapter on ghosts, Fortune called this "breaking the contacts," which I think is a very good description of what you are actually doing in these situations.

The simplest ritual for breaking contacts is called *cord cutting*. You take a number of cords or strings, each representing a negative aspect or negative person from which you want to disengage yourself. One end of each cord you tie to some object—it could be your altar, a post, a tree, a chair, whatever is at hand. The loose ends of these cords you hold in one hand. Visualize these strings or cords representing the bonds linking you with the person who is harassing or attacking you. Once you have fixed this in your imagination, take an edged Magickal Weapon such as your bolline, athame, or sword and, one by one, cut the cords.

Visualize these negative bonds falling away from you, setting you free. Sense the streams of negative energy flowing toward you being disrupted. The knife, athame, or sword is a symbol of your will. This ritual sends a message to your subconscious mind that you are using your will to cut away the impediments in your life. This is just as effective if you do it as a mental exercise; if the psychic attack is perceived by you as a cord, beam of light, and so on, you can imagine yourself cutting it with a Magickal Weapon you created in your mind. For example, you can, in your imagination, arm yourself with a sword, cut the cord, and then imagine cauterizing the end of the cord with a torch. What you are doing here is breaking up the lines of will between you and the psychic assailant.

Pagan authors such as Donald Michael Kraig, Christopher Penczak, as well as Denning and Phillips, all speak of a technique for detecting negative energy called Triangle of Defense. I use Triangle of Defense like this: once you've detected the direction that the negative energy is coming from, stand in the Entering Tranquility posture and face in that direction. Visualize your energy manifesting at your third eye. Most recommend that you visualize this as a violet or a cobalt-blue light. Doing so will help you create the right resonance to make this work. Bring your hands up to your third eye, palms turned away from you, thumbs and first fingers touching and forming a triangle. You hold this triangle over the third eye area. Then step forward with one foot (traditionally this is the left, but Penczak and I use the right) and thrust your hands forward, sending the triangle of energy out to sever the link. Think of this as a variation on the "Push" technique.

Neutralizing Energy Sources

One of the oldest magickal techniques is to employ some physical object or substance to create a link with the person that you intend to attack with magick. Such a link is also known as a point d'appui, point of contact, or a magnetic link. In the first chapter I mentioned that talismans charged with negative energy could be left in your vicinity to facilitate a link between you and your assailant. Later I told you about quantum teleportation, the instant exchange of information from one place to another. This is what makes such links possible. The assailant can also try to acquire personal items from your home to establish such a teleportation link. Objects that have been used for this purpose include:

- Hair combings and nail clippings
- Clothing
- Photos
- Furniture or personal items
- Saliva, seminal fluid, and menstrual blood

It is true that if your enemy gets hold of something of yours, it may allow them to get a feel for your energy and even establish a link between you and them. This practice is related to psychometry, and I've already mentioned how psychometry can affect a sensitive person. Thus it is prudent for you to discreetly dispose of your hair, nail clippings, or cigarette butts if you have concerns about someone "stalking" you. Of course, this can be taken to extremes. I've seen articles and books that advocate elaborate measures such as wiping off your utensils and the edges of your drinking glass in restaurants to rid them of your saliva. Remember that the quantum principle of entanglement explains that you are already linked to everything around you, including your assailant. These things may be used by an assailant as an aid, it is true. Yet they won't create an insurmountable obstacle to your defense.

If you properly develop your defensive abilities, then anyone getting hold of such personal items will certainly wish that they hadn't. If someone takes something of yours, you can take advantage of their possession of that object by creating a link in reverse: you can use the object they took from you as your own point d'appui to facilitate a link to your assailant. This will make it easier for you to channel your defense at them. Thus the object of yours that they went to all that trouble to obtain becomes a chink in *their* armor. I don't waste any time obsessing over whether someone has gotten a strand of my hair. Let them get some and try something with it, and they'll very quickly find out how they are rewarded for their pains. I use the quantum principle that two objects that have been in contact affect one another. I direct my will at my end to the hair at their end. They'll find my defensive energy coming at them right out of that hair in their direction. I think of myself as a "karma accelerator" in such circumstances.

If you find that your psychic assailant has left some sort of object in your way in an attempt to create a point d'appui, remain calm. Opening yourself to fear also opens you to the influences of such things. If the object is found outside, do not bring it into your home. Leave it where it is and make your preparations for neutralizing it. If it is found inside, take it out of your home. Many prefer to use gloves to handle such objects. However, gloves only offer a level of psychological security. They don't offer any true protection from psychic energy.

Place yourself in front of the object. Use a technique such as Entering Tranquility to prepare yourself to deal with the object. Focus your will on the object, charging it with energy to force it to entrain with your intent. Once you have it resonating the way you want it, imagine the stream of energy reversing to the person who put it there. Send it all back to the assailant. If the psychic attacker was using such an object to enhance the creation of a simulacrum or other manifestation, this will shut off the simulacrum's "power source" and cause it to fade away. This is what I meant earlier by *no energy source, no manifestation*.

Once you've neutralized the object with these techniques, place the object in a box of salt for a day or so to ground it out. This will shield it, preventing the person who put it there from re-establishing a link to it. After the object has been grounded, take it apart carefully, stitch by stitch, feather by feather. As you dismantle it, focus on dismantling or disrupting negative energy directed toward you, making the component parts resonate with your peaceful energy. Place the dismantled object in a box and take it away from your house to dispose of it. Traditionally you are supposed to bury such things to dispose of them. A crossroads is typically considered to be an ideal location for doing so, but I don't go out of my way looking for a crossroads to bury things like this.

Old Wives' Tales

TWELVE

Old Wives' Tales

I therefore claim to show, not how men think in myths,
but how myths operate in men's minds
without their being aware of the fact.

—Claude Lévi-Strauss,
The Raw and the Cooked, 1964

Books on psychic self-defense, both new and old, are full of spells, formulas, tinctures, and lists of talismans, amulets, and charms that are supposed to be essential for your safety. These books declare that such magickal defense techniques will work for everyone. Many people purchase such books on Witchcraft or magick and blindly follow the formulas therein. Then they are disappointed when nothing happens. What have they done wrong?

Don't misunderstand me. There are a lot of good books on magick out there. The reason that a technique didn't work for you may well be because the book you bought was written by someone who doesn't know what they are doing. However, it is equally likely that the reason that the technique didn't work for you is that you aren't anything like the author who created that technique. You may find that some techniques in a particular book work for you while others do not. Books of magick are a bit like cookbooks—they will contain some things that you like and that work well and others that do not.

We are all different. What works well for one person may not work as well for another. There are all sorts of things that I copied out of my initiator's Books of Shadows in my early years that don't work for me. Once you have eliminated the possibilities that you've made a mistake or misunderstood the instructions, you can only conclude that perhaps the technique you are using is either basically flawed or at least unsuitable for your talents and abilities. The latter is often the case. Magick that works for someone else doesn't necessarily work as well, if at all, for you.

You should not choose a particular defensive magickal technique based on tradition. Please don't do something because "this is the way that it has always been done." As you will see in a moment, a lot of the "traditional" warding and defensive techniques listed in old books about psychic self-defense are nonsense. You should use a particular technique because it *works*, not because it is an institution. Nietzsche once wrote:

> *Every tradition grows ever more venerable—the more remote its origin, the more confused that origin is. The reverence due to it increases from generation to generation. The tradition finally becomes holy and inspires awe.*[68]

If something doesn't work, toss it out and try something else. Stay in touch with new developments to prevent stagnation of thought. Keep in mind the twelfth Warrior precept from my book *Full Contact Magick:* "Be creative!"

---

68. Friedrich Wilhelm Nietzsche, *Human, All Too Human* (1878), 7.

Before I go on to the lengthy list of things that I've discovered are a waste of time from a psychic self-defense perspective, I want to reinforce what I said earlier on the subject of the elimination of habits and routine. Routines and habits also arise out of traditions and customs. As I noted earlier, a Warrior has no routines. The Warrior must be spontaneous and fluid rather than a creature of habit or tradition.

This does not mean that routines and regimens don't have their place. But you shouldn't become fettered by them; they shouldn't prevent flexibility and innovation. They shouldn't become a liability. If a change is called for, you shouldn't hesitate to change. That's why the thirteenth Warrior precept in *Full Contact Magick* was "Do not engage in useless activity."

If you are a serious student, then along the way you are going to pick up techniques that work from various different sources. You are constantly learning things from new instructors and new books. You experiment. Along the way you will find out what works for you. If you find that something won't work for you at your present stage of development, you set it aside for later. If you find that a particular technique or spell doesn't work, you toss it out. If you find one that does, you put each of these into your "toolbox" for possible later use. That's how I came up with this book. In the end you have something that doesn't necessarily conform entirely to any particular style or tradition. Do not let forms or tradition influence you in these decisions. Bruce Lee once said, "Forms are vain repetitions which offer an orderly and beautiful escape from self-knowledge with an alive opponent."[69]

This said, let's look at some of the traditional methods of psychic self-defense to see how they stand up to modern understanding of magick and quantum theories.

---

69. Bruce Lee, *Tao of Jeet Kune Do*, 16.

There is a mass of urban legends and protective techniques involving talismans, amulets, and various protective substances, baths, and fumigations. Some of these have a foundation in reality. Some of it is "snake oil." If you approach this from the quantum worldview, you quickly see that many things listed as essential to psychic self-defense are simply aids to concentration on the problem at hand. This is the principle of Magickal Weapons that I wrote about in chapter 4. Seeing, smelling, or just being aware of their presence can assist the novice by reminding them of the protection required. Yet I must emphasize that it is *you* who create the protective effect, not your talisman or charm. This means, of course, that if you have any ability at all, you can dispense with such items entirely. Let's look at some of these ancient protective measures to see how effective they really are.

Many of the things that I'm about to list can be thought of as "psychic armor." Armor is one of the oldest means of personal protection. The simple shield, greaves, and helmet of ancient Warriors evolved into chain mail, then into elaborate suits of plate armor, and finally into the modern flexible armor vests worn today by police officers and soldiers. Armor does protect you, but only so much. For every type of armor, there is some form of weapon designed to pierce it. Battlements can be breached, defenses infiltrated. Armor can be helpful, but armor alone can't protect you. You should not rely just on psychic armor for protection.

Sigils

The word *sigil* is derived from the Latin *sigillum* ("seal" or "mark"), a diminutive of *signum* ("sign"). A sigil is a written character that represents a particular force of nature or spirit. In ceremonial magick, a sigil is a design, initial, or device used on a document or object, or traced in the air during invocations and evocations.

Medieval magicians believed that each spirit had a sigil that identified or was related to it, probably because it was common practice in those times for people to have personal seals or sigils that they used to seal letters as a sort of signature.

Common methods of creating sigils included the use of magickal squares. A magickal square is a type of grid of letters. To make a sigil, one traces a line to connect the letters of the name of the spirit, starting with the first letter and continuing in sequence. If the magickal square is numerical, such as a kamea, then one traces the lines between the numbers representing the numerical value of the letters in the name. The Golden Dawn used their symbol of the Rose Cross to make sigils. Each petal of the Rose in this symbol represented a letter in the Hebrew alphabet, and the sigil was traced in a manner similar to that used with magickal squares. Another form of sigil is found in geomancy, which involves examining talismanic or telesmatic figures created by connecting dots on a page.

Norse runes are also often used as sigils. For example, the Elk, Elhaz, or Algiz rune (which looks like an upside-down peace symbol without the circle) is said to work well for warding and psychic self-defense. A charged amulet with this rune, preferably painted red, is traditionally believed to work wonders for personal barriers and peace of mind.

Traditionally, sigils are used to seal gaps in your defenses. Almost any holy symbol that you can imagine has been used for this purpose at some time or another. Christians use the sign of the cross for this purpose all the time.

One of the oldest protective sigils is the pentagram—the five-pointed star, with one point uppermost. This is also known as Solomon's Seal, though other texts assign the name Solomon's Seal to the hexagram instead. Pythagoras referred to the pentagram as the *pentalpha*, since it represents the letter alpha (the letter A) in five different positions. The pentagram is incorporated into the Wiccan pentacle: a pentagram engraved within a round disk of wood, metal, ceramic, or glass. The pentacle is a symbol of both the earth and the Wiccan's understanding of the universe.

The pentagram was regarded by the ancient Greeks as a talisman and preservative from danger, and was inscribed on the threshold of doorways. Early Christians used it as a symbol of the five wounds of Christ. Israel Regardie, in his *The Complete Golden Dawn System of Magic*, referred to it as the Signet Star of the Microcosm, representing the operation of the spirit and the four elements under the presidency of YHShVH (Yesheshuah, Yeheshuah, or Hehovashah—the Pentagrammaton). The Hermetic Order of the Golden Dawn associated this symbol with Mars and with the Hebrew letter Heh. The Golden Dawn called it the Flaming Pentagram, or the Star of the Great Light.

Each of the five points of the pentagram represents one of the five traditional elements: Spirit, Air, Fire, Water, and Earth. As Spirit is represented by the topmost point, this symbol is said to represent the dominion of Spirit over the other four elements and the supremacy of reason over matter.

Many magickal traditions trace the symbol of the pentagram in the air during rituals. As a general rule, one commences by tracing toward the angle of the pentagram that represents the element being invoked, and away from that angle while banishing. Old books on psychic self-defense advocate placing symbols like pentagrams on doors, walls, and windows to provide protection.

Sigils like this do not have any power of their own. The diagram or rune that you've put on the wall or traced in the air isn't what protects you. The thoughts that were in your head when you placed it there are what did the trick. That's right, it's another form of focusing tool, another Magickal Weapon. Tracing a sigil in the air is a ritual gesture that helps focus your thoughts (and your will) on the object of your magick. Of course, as I pointed out earlier, once you've learned to focus properly, you can do so without having to draw symbols like this at all.

Talismans and Amulets

The terms *talisman, telesma,* and *telesmata* come from the French language and are derived from the Arabic *tilsam* ("magic figure" or "horoscope"). They may also be related to the Greek term *telesma* ("incantation"). A talisman is an object believed to have magickal properties. The Hermetic Order of the Golden Dawn referred to them as *telesma.*

Talismans and other sacred objects are often worn to ward off evil influences. This could be a part of a ring, bracelet, necklace, or waist-chain. Old texts indicate that you should prepare the chosen object by cleansing it. You are told to place the object in your strongest hand and place your psychic shield around yourself—an egg-shaped field of intense blue light all around you. Once you feel adequately protected, you are supposed to let your strength and energy surge into the chosen object in your hand, implanting the feeling of your shield onto the object.

Amulets are another traditional form of psychic self-protection. The word *amulet* comes from the French *amulette,* which was derived from the Latin *amuletum* ("a charm"). Doreen Valiente asserts that *amulet* "is probably derived from the Latin *amiolor,* meaning 'I repel, or drive away'."[70] An amulet is a charm, often worn around the neck, that is supposed to bring

---

70. Doreen Valiente, *An ABC of Witchcraft,* 5.

the wearer protection. It may be made of plants, metals, or stones, and it may be inscribed with words or symbols.

Amulets and talismans are another form of Magickal Weapon. As such, they assist us in focusing our attention on our protection. However, like armor, amulets and charms can be overcome, especially if the person wearing one thinks that the protection comes from the object and not from their mind. There is only so much energy stored in them (assuming that there is any at all). Yet this point is completely overlooked in most texts that describe them. As is true for sigils, talismans and amulets are simply aids for focusing your will, which is something you can learn to do very well without them.

Iron is supposed to have a protective effect as a talisman. Grasping or wearing an iron object is said to confer protection. Here is an example of Norse protective magick involving iron: Take a large iron or steel nail or a railroad spike. Hold it and imagine it filling with blue light. Next, invoke the God Thor and ask that justice be done, telling Thor who you are angry at and why. When this iron is charged, pound it into the ground near the miscreant's home or place of business.

Look at this process carefully. It isn't the iron that is protecting you. This procedure involves concentrating protective energy into the iron spike. It is the magician charging the object, not the object, that creates the effect.

Garlic is one of the most common elements of protective amulets. Fans of horror literature or Hollywood horror movies have heard of the supposedly protective qualities of garlic. Garlic is traditionally reputed to have magickal properties and to be an effective ward against vampires and other creatures of the night. Onions are said to be useful for this purpose, too. Many texts say that garlic and onions absorb negative energy. You're told to peel and slice garlic cloves or onions and place them around your rooms in saucers or on pieces of paper overnight to absorb negative energy. Folklore tells us that if the garlic or onion turns black overnight, it shows that negative influences were absorbed. You're told that every day you should remove the used garlic or onion and either bury it, burn it outdoors, or flush it down the toilet. Whatever you do, you are not supposed to use this garlic or onion for cooking after you've used it this way.

OK, people. If this were true, then you'd better stop cooking with garlic and onions altogether and give up foods containing them, because the garlic and onions in your pantry or on the supermarket shelves have been sitting around soaking up negative energy all day, every day since they left the farm. Again, look at the process involved: you're going around deliberately setting up garlic "energy traps" around the house. The garlic has become a Magickal Weapon to focus intent. I certainly use onions and garlic in cooking: they're flavorful and have many health benefits. I don't use them for self-defense. I can think of better ways to focus my intentions than strewing vegetables around the house.

I don't know about you, but I don't like the idea of objects of any sort sitting around in my house storing up negative energy. I don't want my house littered with storage devices full of toxic energy. My approach is to prevent the negative stuff from getting anywhere near me or my house in the first place. I want the negative stuff out there, not in here where I am.

Many other substances are traditionally said to absorb negative influences. For example:

- Eggs are supposed to absorb negative energy. Rubbing your body with an egg is supposed to absorb negativity. Placing an egg by the bed or in each room is supposed to absorb negative energy. After a week you take these eggs and bury them. They are not to be eaten afterward. Burying an egg outside your front door is also supposed to provide protection. I feel the same way about eggs as I do about garlic and onions: if this folklore about eggs were true, then the eggs in your refrigerator and in the cooler at the supermarket are becoming contaminated by negative energy as you read this. The truth is that these eggs are simply being used as a focusing tool in these applications. Eggs are more effective when used to make omelettes than when they're used for psychic self-defense.

- Oils are also traditionally believed to provide shielding against negative energy. Oils recommended for this purpose include white sandalwood, lavender, frankincense, lemon, myrrh, and deer's tongue. Oils said to assist grounding include myrrh, cypress, and moss. Yet it is the intent that you focus on their application or that is brought to mind by their scent that is the real source of the protection involved.

Fumigation

Fumigation has historically been used as a defense against evil influences. Garlic is one of the most common substances traditionally used in fumigation for protection. One technique involves mixing garlic juice with water and evaporating this mixture in an oil burner for fragrant essential oils. Part of the underlying truth behind these myths is the smell of garlic: it certainly does drive people away.

Fumigation is not a technique that I'd recommend. I confess that using substances such as incense isn't my thing: doing so plays hell with my allergies, and if you've got allergies it probably causes you problems, too. The pungent smells involved in most protective fumigation techniques will repel humans more easily than any "astral wildlife." An ancient alternative to fumigating with garlic involves rubbing the skin with garlic juice. The feet and hands are the recommended sites. Doing so will cause you to exude a garlic odor that supposedly repels evil influences. It certainly repels friends and neighbors.

Other substances historically used as fumigants to repel negative energies include:

- *Sulfur*—This is actually one of the active ingredients that makes garlic effective for other purposes. ***The danger with using sulfur is that burning it generates poisonous smoke,*** so if you insist upon using it, it must be used with great care. It should be used in small quantities and you should not remain in the room while it is being fumigated. Stay out of the room for at least half an hour and thoroughly air out the room afterward. Don't forget to remove your pets from the area—burning sulfur will kill pets, even goldfish. It is far better not to use it at all.

- *Vinegar*—Dishes of vinegar distributed around the house are believed to absorb negative energy. It is said to work even better if you dissolve some camphor in the vinegar. If this were true, then the vinegar you purchase at the supermarket is already contaminated, having absorbed the negative energy of everyone that passed the store shelf before you got there. Vinegar (mild acetic acid) *is* a useful substance for cleaning the house, which is, as I said earlier, part of keeping negative energy out of your home. Other than that, I don't use vinegar in psychic self-defense at all.

- *Nitric Acid*—Dion Fortune recommended a dilute solution of nitric acid in her book *Psychic Self-Defence*. This is reputed to be stronger than onions, garlic, or vinegar. It's strong, all right; the problem is that it is *very* caustic and therefore *very* dangerous to use. I'd rather you didn't.

· *Indian fumigants*—A mixture of hot chili peppers, garlic, and ginger is recommended in an Indian system of magick, Punja. You need to be careful with this as the smoke can irritate your eyes and lungs. Use the same precautions as for the use of sulfur. Better yet, don't use it at all.

· *Rosemary*—Supposed to have strong repellent properties. A rosemary bush is said to be particularly effective, and rosemary bushes planted around the house are said to offer protection. Yet it is actually the intent that goes into the planting of the bush that really offers the protection (yes, it is another focusing tool). Vervain and sage are reputed to have similar properties. I don't use rosemary or sage for psychic self-defense. I use them when cooking poultry.

· *Hawthorn*—Supposed to dispel negativity if you put it in corners of rooms and under furniture. You're supposed to replace the hawthorn sprigs after every vacuuming. Rather than rummaging around under the couch for old hawthorn sprigs, I'll rely on psychic self-defense techniques that don't involve bits of prickly bushes, thanks.

All fumigation really does is put a smell in the air that reminds you that you're supposed to be protected, which in turn causes you to focus energy on that defensive task. There's that idea of an aid to focusing your will again. These items all become focusing tools.

Water

There's a great deal of folklore about the value of running water as a barrier to negative influences. Some writers claim that water can provide an insurmountable barrier to nasty psychic wildlife. They recommend installing ion generators in your house, as well as sprinklers, fountains, and other water features. They may even suggest using your shower or a pot of water on the stove to generate steam. Traditionally, putting a glass of water above your bed or on a nightstand by your bed is supposed to absorb negative energy. Adding salt, lemon juice, or a camphor mothball is said to enhance its effect. You are not supposed to drink this or water plants with it afterward. One Internet article on psychic self-defense that I encountered actually recommended placing a plastic garden hose full of water around the house as a barrier against psychic attack.

Near running water or ocean surf, the air is full of ions released from the water that have a positive effect on one's health. This is why ion generators work, and this is part of the basis for the legends about the protective value of water. I've certainly noticed that when I get away from the Greater Vancouver area to the islands in the Strait of Georgia I feel isolated from the negative energy by the seaside, but a lot of this is because I'm now miles and miles away from all that hectic urban energy back home. I wouldn't say that water is a perfect barrier, but it can help. You can use the steam or vapor to help you visualize cleaning away negative energy from your surroundings. I mentioned grounding exercises involving baths earlier. These also emit useful ions.

Large bodies of water do have an effect, if only to distance you from the source of the negative energy. The larger a body of water, the better an "energy sink" it is. I don't rely on rivers, streams, ditches, or garden hoses providing any effective protection against psychic attack on their own. If they help you define the boundaries that you set up around yourself, well and good. Save the garden hose for watering your lawn and garden.

Fire

Likewise there are many customs involving the use of fire for protection. Leaping over the flames of bonfires or going between fires is an ancient curative and protective measure. As I suggested in my description of meditation exercises earlier in this book, using flame as a focal point for concentration is very useful. I'm very fond of meditating on flames. Yet the fire itself is just a focal point. It doesn't protect in and of itself. It doesn't burn away the connections in a psychic attack.

Salt and Crystals

Salt, crystals, and precious stones are also traditionally believed to provide protection from psychic attack. Sprinkling sea salt on your mattress under the sheets is supposed to ground you and absorb energy. This is said to be particularly important if you sleep on a waterbed. Some authors advocate placing a circle of salt around your bed or house in order to shield it.

Of course all crystals have particular frequencies with which they resonate. I wrote in an earlier chapter about entrainment and how things tend to synchronize their oscillations or vibrations when brought into contact. Through entrainment, salt and other crystalline substances can help alter the negative energy of objects brought into contact with them. That's why I recommended placing a point d'appui found in your house in a box full of salt: it helps ground out the negative energy. Traditionally, clear quartz, rose quartz, bloodstone, and amber are believed to clear the atmosphere of negative energy. Hematite, onyx, and jet are said to facilitate grounding. Tiger's eye and black tourmaline are believed to help strengthen one's aura.

Putting a line of salt around you or your house isn't going to keep negative energy away from you. It is a two-dimensional circle that you've created with your line of salt, and that's a four-dimensional attack coming at you. As I showed you in the previous chapter, you need to defend yourself with a three-dimensional protective sphere, not a two-dimensional circle. The circle drawn or traced on the ground is simply a visual aid helping you to create this energetic sphere.

Energy Traps

Over the years various "traps" have been manufactured to "capture" or "contain" negative influences. Indian dream catchers are a more elaborate example of such a device. One example I've encountered in my studies involves lining the entire interior of a box with unbroken mirrors. In this box you place an object from the negative person, such as a business card, gift, or any object they have left on your property. You are then supposed to bury the box away from your home. A crossroads is said to be a good location for this purpose, as it is believed to dissipate negative energies quickly.

Do you see the active principle here? Yes, it is another focusing tool. In fact, if you are putting something belonging to the psychic assailant in a box, it is a point d'appui. If you want to go to all the trouble of making a focusing tool like this box, stay concentrated and mindful on what you are doing. Do not let yourself become distracted. As you place the point d'appui object in the box, focus on this object trapping and neutralizing the negative energy being directed to you. When you bury it, stay focused on letting go of the negativity and leaving it behind.

The idea is to have this object attract all that negative energy that was being directed at you. If you do not have an object from the psychic assailant, just keep your focus on "the person or people who wish me ill" and mentally place their energy in the box. An alternative is to visualize "mirrors" facing away from your living space that return any negative energy back to its source. I don't like this technique. It is too much like mirroring and binding, neither of which I'd recommend as psychic self-defense techniques. Let me take a moment now to explain why.

Mirroring

One of the most common traditional psychic self-defense techniques is what I call mirroring. Ronald Eppich calls this technique "visualized protection." It involves visualizing yourself surrounded in a bubble of light or reflective surface that reflects the attack back at the aggressor. You relax and quiet your mind, thinking in ideas rather than in words. You then define the space of the effect; this "reflective surface" needn't extend out any further than the surface of your skin.

For example, you imagine yourself wearing armor. You can use whatever type of armor is most easily visualized. The type is immaterial—medieval plate or mail, Japanese Samurai armor, Kevlar, whatever. Imagine yourself enclosed by this armor. Imagine this armor as having a highly polished reflective surface. See it reflecting any negative energy that is being thrown at you back at its source.

I call this mirroring technique a "karma accelerator," an idea I mentioned in my earlier Warrior books. Your assailant gets their negative energy right back. You're not doing anything negative that will cause you karmic debts yourself. Any harm the assailant receives from getting their negative energy back in their face is their concern. They created the situation, and now they have to live with the consequences. Mirroring is a passive defense technique. One author recommends imaging the *inside* of one's mirrored "shield" as a mirrored surface containing or reflecting back one's own energy, leaving no energy "signature" that an enemy could detect—a sort of "stealth" mode.[71]

Mirroring does work, but I don't like it because the psychic assailant you are sending all this negative energy back to may perceive this negative energy coming back at them as an aggressive act on *your* part rather than the passive act that it is. It doesn't matter that you didn't intend harm to the person you are sending this negative energy back to. That's not the way that it will look at the psychic assailant's end. This may motivate them to fling even more negativity in your direction, because they are going to think that is what *you* are doing. It may also cause them to enlist other people to their cause. These additional people may cause problems for you outside of the magickal realm. In other words, the situation may escalate.

Another consideration is that your aura is actually pierced from within by the fear and/or desire created by the psychic influence directed at you by the assailant. To do this attackers must fill themselves with the emotion of hate or lust to instill fear in you, the victim. If the assailant cannot connect with the victim, then these forces acting through them dam up or rebound. Of course, you using a mirroring technique to defend yourself will certainly result in the energy rebounding. These emotions may build up inside the assailant, which could make them even more hostile toward you than they were to begin with.

A more effective technique, suggested by author Joseph Rinoza Plazo, is to send a psychic message to the assailant to make them feel the way you want or to view things from your

---

71. Jordsvin, "Basic Magickal Protection & Psychic Self-Defense" (accessed 12 February 2007).

standpoint. This is a variation on the visualization techniques one might use in healing another person. Plazo suggests building a "win-win scenario."[72] Often the person attacking you is enraged, even if they are not conscious of attacking you. One technique suggested by Dale Power[73] is called Empathic Field Generation, and it requires you to draw away the attacker's anger, thereby removing the motivation to attack you.

I'm not opposed to these approaches, but as they don't change the assailant's environment or situation, they may not have a lasting effect. If the assailant's frustrations and anger stem from their environment or situation, then simply defusing their frustration isn't a guarantee that the situation or adverse environment won't build their frustrations back up again. If you're not careful, drawing away the intense emotions from a disturbed individual may fill you up with these emotions and cause you all kinds of problems. You need to be secure in your practice of magick before you attempt techniques like these.

As I noted earlier, it is best to keep things simple when defending yourself. Many of the things that I've just described are simply focusing tools, if not very good ones. You don't need a lot of paraphernalia to defend yourself against psychic attacks. What you do need is to hone your skills and learn how to detect and use energy. If you can accomplish this, you will have everything that you need to deal with psychic assailants.

---

72. Joseph Rinoza Plazo, "Psychic Self-Defense," http://www.psychic101 .com/self-defense-psychic.html (accessed 12 February 2007).

73. Dale Power, "Psychic Self Defense in Real Life, "Cherry Sage, http://www .cherrysage.com/articles/TitleLink.php?nId=22 (accessed 22 October 2007).

Conclusion

Conclusion

Out of this nettle, danger, we pluck this flower, safety.

—Shakespeare, *Henry IV, Part 1*

As I pointed out earlier in this book when discussing development of intuition, most people don't ever develop their psychic abilities. In fact, many people have a complete lack of sensitivity to the negative energy around them. Oddly enough, this lack of ability and sensitivity confers a slight measure of natural immunity to psychic attack for some people. This doesn't mean that negative energy doesn't affect such people; it means that this negative atmosphere usually doesn't affect them too severely. What effects they do experience they usually attribute to ill health or stress.

Some people are of course more naturally sensitive than others. Obviously I am not telling you to ignore the negative energy that is directed at you. It may not have a serious effect, but the effects never go away and they do become a chronic annoyance. Negative energy will have a negative effect on you.

A little attention to your psychic safety can vastly improve your situation.

If you do nothing but sit and dwell on your misfortune, you'll only make it worse. As you have seen, destructive magick often relies on fear to get an effective hold on you. If you don't fear it, it won't work as well. Now that you've got this book, you'll be able to develop the skills and confidence to deal with psychic attacks. This confidence will make it less likely that you'll succumb to fear if you are attacked.

I've shown you how to give yourself psychic armor while at the same time showing you that relying on such armor alone is not sufficient. Armor and defenses can be overcome. Wards provide protection, and you should not be without them. Police officers don't leave the station without their personal body armor, but they don't rely on this alone to provide protection. The armor is simply insurance to cover situations in which they may have overlooked something. Armor reduces the possible consequences of these oversights.

Nor am I saying that you should hurl thunderbolts at people who direct negative energy at you. Just because they are trying to harm you with their negative energy doesn't mean that you will improve the situation by firing negative energy back. Remember how I told you earlier about the reduction of crime in a city just by putting positive energy out there? You get back what you put out.

Psychic self-defense is all about developing an awareness of the energies that surround you. Developing sensitivity to your own energy helps you use it for many different purposes. Developing sensitivity to energy that surrounds you helps you to manipulate that energy to your advantage. This book has shown you how to raise and direct energy for your defense. When an assailant directs energy at you, you now know how to block it, ground it, deflect it, "push" it, or "pull" it. You use the attacker against himself.

Once you have developed your mastery of the magickal techniques in this book, you will be able to use your will to neutralize any negative influences thrown in your direction. You'll do this almost automatically, without having to resort to casting Circles or setting up defenses.

By now, hopefully you'll have a simple understanding of quantum principles such as entanglement and entrainment, giving you a better understanding of how magick works. This book will also have shown you how to clear out the outdated clutter and simplify your practice of magick. Magick is causing change in conformity with your will. The observer affects what is observed.

You've learned the importance of maintaining a positive attitude and taking charge of your life. This book has shown you how to find your strengths and use them effectively to empower yourself without inviting negative energy into your life. You've learned that the key to a strong defense is a strong will and self-discipline.

The many books of magick and psychic self-defense out there are full of spells, talismans, amulets, potions, and magickal paraphernalia that they tell you will protect you from harm. I hope you now realize that it isn't any of these objects or potions that actually protect you. They are all just Magickal Weapons. It is your mastery of these Magickal Weapons that protects you, not the objects at all. Ultimately, it all comes down to self-mastery. Master yourself, and everything else in your life will take care of itself. You really don't need anything other than what you came into this world with to defend yourself from psychic attack.

I've shown you how to use the concept of Magickal Artillery to use the five principles of the Witch's Pyramid to enhance your magick. To Know is the base from which your magick is launched. To Keep Silent is scanning your environment to identify any threats that need to be dealt with. To Dare is loading yourself up with the psychic defensive charge that you want to send out. To Imagine is setting your sights on the target of your magick. To Will is pulling the trigger and letting the magick fly.

Eventually you'll be able to go through life without being consciously aware of your protective wards. Like me, you will have developed your personal defenses to the point where you won't need any Magickal Weapons to assist you in everyday situations. Master the techniques in this book and most of the negative stuff tossed in your direction will bounce off without you even having to think about defending yourself from the chaotic world out there.

Bibliography

Bibliography

Articles and Lectures

Barney, Natalie Clifford. Quoted in "Gods," in *Adam*, N. 299. London: Adam Books, 1962.

Barrie, J. M. Rectorial address at St. Andrew's University, St. Andrews, Scotland, 3 May 1922.

Beckwith, Carol, and Angela Fisher. "Masai Passage to Manhood," *National Geographic* magazine, vol. 196, no. 3, September 1999.

Bell, J. S. "On the Problem of Hidden Variables in Quantum Mechanics," *Review of Modern Physics*, vol. 38, issue 3, July 1966, 447–452.

Bohm, David. "Consciousness and Self-Consciousness—A Working Paper," *Psychological Perspectives,* vol. 38, C. G. Jung Institute of Los Angeles, Spring–Summer 1988.

——. "Beyond Relativity and Quantum Mechanics," *Psychological Perspectives*, vol. 38, C. G. Jung Institute of Los Angeles, Spring–Summer 1988.

Bruce, Robert. "Developing Natural Resistance to the Negatives of Life," Astral Dynamics website. http://www.astraldynamics.com/tutorials?BoardID=10&BulletinID=215 (accessed 17 October 2007).

——. "White Light Shields," Astral Dynamics website. http://www.astraldynamics.com/tutorials/?BoardID=10&BulletinID=214 (accessed 17 October 2007).

Charboneau-Harrison, Karen. "Psychic Self Defense," http://www.isisbooks.com/psyselfdef.asp (accessed 17 October 2007).

Curott, Phyllis. "Exploding Wiccan Dogma." Lecture at Blessed Be and Merry Meet in DC (BBMMDC) conference in Washington D.C., 14 October 2000.

Davidson, Aharon. "Tachyonic Compactification," *Physical Review D*, vol. 35, issue 6, 15 March 1987.

Eppich, Ronald. "Psychic Self-Defense: Protection for the Body, Mind and Soul," http://www.shamans-cave.com/Psychic_Self_Defense.html (accessed 13 February 2007).

Goldberg, Dr. Bruce. "Psychic Self Defense," http://www.drbrucegoldberg.com/defense.htm (accessed 12 February 2007).

Herbert, Nick. "Notes Toward A User's Guide to the Quantum Connection," *Psychological Perspectives*, vol. 38, C. G. Jung Institute of Los Angeles, Spring–Summer 1988.

Jordsvin. "Basic Magickal Protection & Psychic Self-Defense," http://www.wicca.com/celtic/wicca/defense.htm (acccessed 12 February 2007).

Le Guin, Ursula K. "Winged: The Creatures on My Mind," in *Harper's* magazine, August 1990.

Palmer, Jeffry R., PhD. "The Nature of Thought Energy," Project Sanctuary, http://projectsanctuary.com/main/modules.php?name=News&file=article&sid=58 (accessed 12 November 2005).

Plazo, Joseph Rinoza. "Psychic 101 Psychic Self-Defense," http://www.psychic101.com/self-defense-psychic.html (accessed 12 November 2005).

Power, Dale. "Psychic Self Defense in Real Life," Cherry Sage, http://www.cherrysage.com/articles/TitleLink.php?nId=22 (accessed 17 October 2007).

Price, Brian R. "A Code of Chivalry: Modern, Based on the 'Old Code'," http://www.chronique.com/Library/Chivalry/code .htm, April 1997 (accessed 17 October 2007).

Randolph, Keith. "Psychic Self Defense," The Llewellyn Encyclopedia, http://www.llewellynencyclopedia.com/article/271 (accessed 13 February 2007).

Sanguinarius. "Alternative Methods for Psychic Self-Defense," http://www.sanguinarius.org/articles/tvp-altmeth.shtml (accessed 17 October 2007).

Slater, Kate. "Hearing Voices," position paper on Drawing Down, 1994.

Steinem, Gloria. "Far From the Opposite Shore," in *Ms.* magazine (July 1978 and July/August 1982). Reprinted in *Outrageous Acts and Everyday Rebellions*. New York: Henry Holt, 1983.

Telesco, Patricia. "Psychic Self Defense For Festivals (and Beyond)," 28 August 2002, http://www.witchvox.com/va/ dt_va.html?a=usny&c=festtips&id=4661 (accessed 17 October 2007).

Walker, Evan H. "The Complete Quantum Mechanical Anthropologist." Report presented at the 73rd annual American

Anthropological Association meeting, Mexico City, November 19–24, 1974.

———. "The Nature of Consciousness," *Mathematical Biosciences* 7 (1970), 131–138.

Walker, Evan H., and Nick Herbert. "Hidden Variables: Where Physics and the Paranormal Meet," in *Future Science*, ed. by John White and Stanley Krippner. Garden City, NY: 1977.

Books

Andrews, Ted. *Psychic Protection*. Jackson, TN: Dragonhawk Publishing, 1998.

Ayto, John. *Dictionary of Word Origins*. New York: Arcade, 1990.

Bachelard, Gaston. *The Poetics of Reverie*. Boston: Beacon Press, 1971.

Bacon, Francis. *The Advancement of Learning*. New York: Colonial Press, 1900.

Barnhart, Robert K., ed. *Barnhart Dictionary of Etymology*. New York: H. W. Wilson, 1988.

Belanger, Michelle. *The Psychic Vampire Codex*. York Beach, ME: Red Wheel Weiser, 2004.

Bergson, Henri. *Matter and Memory*. New York: Zone Books, 1988.

Bergson, Henri (trans. by Mabelle Andison). *The Creative Mind*. New York: Greenwood Press, 1968.

Bernanos, Georges. *The Last Essays of Georges Bernanos*. New York: Greenwood Press, 1968.

Bierce, Ambrose. *The Devil's Dictionary*. New York: Dover, 1993.

Blacking, John. *How Musical is Man?* Seattle: University of Washington Press, 1973.

Blamires, Steve. *Glamoury: Magic of the Celtic Green World*. St. Paul, MN: Llewellyn, 1995.

Bohm, David. *Wholeness and the Implicate Order*. London: ARK Paperbacks, 1983.

Bohm, David, and David Peat. *Science, Order and Creativity*. New York: Bantam, 1987.

Bolitho, William. *Twelve Against the Gods*. New York: Simon & Schuster, 1929.

Bradley, F. H. *Appearance and Reality: A Metaphysical Essay*. Oxford, UK: Clarendon Press, 1951.

Brown, Norman O. *Love's Body*. Berkeley, CA: University of California Press, 1990.

Carlyle, Thomas. *Sartor Resartus*. New York: A. L. Burt Co., 1833–34.

Castaneda, Carlos. *Journey to Ixtlan*. New York: Pocket Books, 1974.

———. *Tales of Power*. Markham, ON: Simon & Schuster, 1974.

Cooley, Charles Horton. *Human Nature and the Social Order*. Glencoe, IL: Free Press, 1956.

Crowley, Aleister. *Magick In Theory and Practice*. New York: Castle Books, 1976.

Cunningham, Scott. *Wicca: A Guide for the Solitary Practitioner*. St. Paul, MN: Llewellyn, 1989.

Davies, Robertson. *What's Bred in the Bone*. Ashland, OR: Blackstone Audio Books, 1985.

De Givry, Grillot. *Witchcraft, Magic and Alchemy*. New York: Frederick Publications, 1954.

De Laurence, L. W., ed. *The Greater Key of Solomon*. Mokelumne Hill, CA: Health Research, 1914.

Denning, Melita, and Osborne Phillips. *Practical Guide to Psychic Self Defense & Well-Being*. St. Paul, MN: Llewellyn, 1987.

Dhammananda, Sri K. *Meditation: The Only Way*. Kuala Lumpur: Buddhist Missionary Society, 1987.

Duc de la Rochefoucauld, François. *Sentences et Maximes Morales*. (First published in 1665.) New York: Random House, 1959.

Emerson, Ralph Waldo. "Books" from *Society and Solitude*. Boston: Fields, Osgood & Co., 1870.

———. *Works*. Cambridge, MA: Belknap Press, 1971.

Farrar, Stewart. *What Witches Do: The Modern Coven Revealed*. New York: Coward, McCann & Geoghegan, 1971.

Farrar, Janet, and Stewart Farrar. *A Witches Bible, Volume II: The Rituals*. New York: Magickal Childe, 1984.

Fitch, Ed. *Magical Rites from the Crystal Well*. St. Paul, MN: Llewellyn Publications, 1988.

Fitzgerald, Penelope. *The Gate of Angels*. London: Collins, 1990.

Fortune, Dion. *Moon Magic*. York Beach, ME: Samuel Weiser, 1978.

———. *Psychic Self-Defence*. Wellingborough, UK: The Aquarian Press, 1981.

Frank, Philipp. *Einstein: His Life and Times*. Boston: Beacon Press, 1950.

Gibran, Kahlil. *A Second Treasury of Kahlil Gibran*, New York: Citadel Press, 1962.

Haldane, J. B. S. "God-Makers" from *The Inequality of Man and Other Essays*. London: Chatto & Windus, 1932.

Hall, Judy. *The Art of Psychic Protection*. York Beach, ME: Samuel Weiser, 1997.

Hamilton-Parker, Craig. *Protecting the Soul: Safeguarding Your Spiritual Journey*. New York: Sterling, 2003.

Harrow, Judy. "Basics for Beginners," Protean Book of Shadows, Proteus Coven, 1993.

Hart, Mickey. *Drumming at the Edge of Magic*. New York: HarperSanFrancisco, 1990.

Havel, Václav. *Disturbing the Peace*. Knopf, New York: Knopf, 1990.

Hawking, Stephen. *A Brief History of Time: From the Big Bang to Black Holes*. New York: Bantam, 1988.

———. *The Universe in a Nutshell*. New York: Bantam, 2001.

Heinlein, Robert A. *Stranger in a Strange Land*. New York: Ace Books, 1987.

Heraclitus (trans. by Guy Davenport). *Herakleitos & Diogenes*. Bolinas, CA: Grey Fox Press, 1976.

Herbert, George. *Jacula Prudentum*. London: printed by T. Maxey for T. Garthwait, 1651.

Hine, Phil. *Condensed Chaos*. Tempe, AZ: New Falcon, 1995.

Hutton, Ronald. *Triumph of the Moon*. Oxford, UK: Oxford University Press, 1999.

Huxley, Thomas Henry. *Collected Essays*. New York: Macmillan, 1925.

Johnson, Samuel. *The History of Rasselas*. Oxford, UK: Clarendon Press, 1929.

K, Amber. *True Magick: A Beginner's Guide*. St. Paul, MN: Llewellyn, 1990.

Klagsburn, Francine, ed. *The First Ms. Reader*. New York: Warner Books, 1972.

Konstantinos. *Vampires: The Occult Truth*. St. Paul, MN: Llewellyn, 2003.

Lampert, Vanessa. *Practical Kabbalah for Magic and Protection*. New York: Friedman Fairfax, 2002.

Lee, Bruce. *Tao of Jeet Kune Do*. Santa Clarita, CA: Ohara Publications, 1975.

Lévi, Eliphas. *Transcendental Magic*. (First published in 1896.) New York: Samuel Weiser, 1974.

Libet, Benjamin, and Stephen M. Kosslyn. *Mind Time: The Temporal Factor in Consciousness*. Cambridge, MA: Harvard University Press, 2004.

Luc Vauvenargues, Marquis de. *Réflexions et Maximes*. Paris: Croville, 1746.

Madden, Kristin. *Pagan Parenting: Spiritual, Magical, & Emotional Development of the Child*. St. Paul, MN: Llewellyn, 2000.

Mayne, Jonathan. *The Mirror of Art*. London: Phaidon, 1965.

Merzbacher, Eugene. *Quantum Mechanics*. New York: John Wiley and Sons, 1967.

Millman, Dan. *Way of the Peaceful Warrior*. Tiburon, CA: H. J. Kramer, 1980.

Mitchell, Dr. Edgar, and Dwight Williams. *The Way of the Explorer*. New York: G. P. Putnam's Sons, 1996.

Moore, Robert, and Douglas Gillette. *King, Warrior, Magician, Lover: Rediscovering the Archetypes of the Mature Masculine*. New York: HarperSanFrancisco, 1990.

———. *The Warrior Within: Accessing the Knight in the Male Psyche*. New York: HarperSanFrancisco, 1992.

Musashi, Miyamoto. *The Book of Five Rings*. New York: Bantam, 1988.

Nelson, Portia. *There's a Hole in My Sidewalk*. Hillsboro, OR: Beyond Words Publishing, 1977.

O'Gaea, Ashleen, and Carol Garr. *Circles Behind Bars: A Complete Handbook for the Incarcerated Witch*. Unpublished. [2000].

Penczak, Christopher. *The Witch's Shield: Protection Magick & Psychic Self-Defense*. St. Paul, MN: Llewellyn, 2004.

Rabelais, Francois. *Gargantua and Pantagruel*. Boston: Houghton, 1940.

Radin, Dr. Dean. *Entangled Minds: Extrasensory Experiences in a Quantum Reality*. New York: Pocket Books, 2006.

Ramsland, Katherine. *Piercing the Darkness: Undercover with Vampires in America Today*. San Francisco: HarperPrism, 1998.

RavenWolf, Silver. *Silver's Spells for Protection*. St. Paul, MN: Llewellyn, 2000.

Reich-Ranicki, Marcel (trans. by Ralph Manheim). *Thomas Mann and His Family*. London: Collins, 1989.

Rosenberg, Harold. *The Tradition of the New*. New York: Horizon Press, 1960.

Shakespeare, William (Stanley Wells and Gary Taylor, eds). *William Shakespeare: The Complete Works*. Oxford, UK: Clarendon Press, 1988.

Shaw, George Bernard (1856–1950). "Maxims for Revolutionists: Liberty and Equality," from *Man and Superman*. New York: Chelsea House, 1987.

Stevens, Wallace. "The Necessary Angel," from the *Columbia Dictionary of Quotations*. New York: Columbia University Press, 1951.

Stewart, R. J. *Celtic Gods, Celtic Goddesses*. London: Blandford, 1990.

Thondup, Tulku. *Boundless Healing: Meditation Exercises to Enlighten the Mind and Heal the Body*. Boston: Shambhala, 2000.

Thoreau, Henry David. *Walden*. (First published in 1854.) New York: Dover, 1985.

——. *Journals*. Boston: Houghton Mifflin, 1906.

Thurber, James (Michael J. Rosen, ed.). *Collecting Himself: James Thurber on Writing and Writers, Humor, and Himself*. New York: Harper & Row, 1989.

Twain, Mark. (Paul Baender, ed.). *What is Man?* New York: De Vinne Press, 1973.

——. *Following the Equator and Other Anti-Imperialist Essays*. New York: Oxford University Press, 1996.

Tzu, Sun (trans. by Thomas Cleary). *The Art of War*. Boston: Shambhala, 1991.

Valiente, Doreen. *Witchcraft For Tomorrow*. Custer, WA: Phoenix Publishing, 1978.

Waite, A. E. *The Book of Black Magic and Ceremonial Magic*. New York: Causeway Books, 1973.

Walker, Barbara G. *The Woman's Encyclopedia of Myths and Secrets*. San Francisco: HarperCollins, 1983.

Watkins, Calvert, ed. *The American Heritage Dictionary of Indo-European Roots* (revised). Boston: Houghton Mifflin, 1985.

Wong, Kiew Kit. *Chi Kung: For Health and Vitality*. Shaftesbury, UK: Element Books, 1997.

Wood, Robin. *When, Why . . . If*. Dearborn, MI: Livingtree, 1996.

Websites

http://www.aiis.com.au The Ashish Institute for Inner Studies (accessed 7 November 2007).

http://www.wicca.com/celtic/wicca/defense.htm "Basic Magickal Protection & Psychic Self-Defense" by Erik Herne and The Celtic Connection (accessed 7 November 2007).

http://www.spirit-of-yggdrasil.com/page346.aspx "Spirit of Yggdrasil" by Ormungandr (accessed 18 October 2006).

http://www.pranichealing-uk.co.uk/pranic_psychic_self _defence_training.html "Pranic Healing and Psychic Self-Defence" (accessed 5 January 2007).

http://www.psychic101.com/self-defense-psychic.html "Psychic 101 Psychic Self-Defense" (accessed 18 October 2007).

http://www.pathcom.com/~newmoon/defence.htm "Psychic Self-Defense: Tower of Light" (accessed 15 February 2007).

Index

A

accidents, 48, 118
action, 15, 39, 51, 57, 63–64, 69, 78–79, 112, 119
Aikido, 13
Air (element), 60, 89, 106
aggression, 3–5, 9, 68, 179–180
ajna chakra, 104–105
alcohol, 7, 35–36, 43, 126, 132
Algiz, 168
alpha frequencies, 93, 169
altar, 52, 61, 63, 158
altered states, 35
ambush, 24–25
amulets, 8, 164, 167–168, 170–171, 186
Anahata, 104–105
anger, 9, 12, 15, 117, 132–133, 156–157, 171, 181
anxiety, xvi, 2, 7, 11, 19, 31, 125
archetype, 63, 107, 117
armor, 13, 73, 160, 167, 171, 179, 185
artificial elementals, 98, 121
Aspect, Alain, 79
aspect, 26, 40, 84, 158
assailant, x, xvi, 2–3, 8–9, 15, 19, 32, 34, 36, 46–47, 51–53, 57–59, 63, 69, 74, 95, 121, 127–128, 140–141, 146, 150, 155–156, 158–161, 178–181, 185
assessment, 19
astral lights, 121
astral projection, 74, 110
astral temple, 71–74, 119
Athame, 58, 60, 152, 158
auditory effects, 14

AUM, 89, 91
aura, 11, 119, 136, 143, 146, 177, 180
awareness, xv, 7–12, 15, 17–20, 24–26, 28–36, 40–44, 46–47, 50, 55, 69, 75, 84, 98, 100, 106, 156, 164, 167, 185, 187

B

baihui, 104
banishing, 99, 119–120, 169
barrier, 7, 168, 175–176
bath, 136
batteries, xvii, 64, 99
bell, 14
Bell, John, 79
Belanger, Michelle, 109, 111
Berendt, Joachim-Ernst, 88
Berman, Dick, 23
beta frequencies, 39, 93
bhramari breathing, 91–92
Bias, Clifford, 28
Big Bang, 84
binding, 54, 104–105, 141, 179
bindu, 104–105
bioentanglement, 82
Black Veil, the, 111
Blamires, Steve, 59–60
blockages, 103–105, 108, 111, 122, 125, 130, 142–143, 147, 155, 186
body memory, 20
Bohm, David, 55
bolline, 158
Book of Shadows, 74, 165
Bose-Einstein condensates, 82
boundaries, 147–148, 152, 176
Bradley, Marion Zimmer, 73

break the contact, 119
Bruce, Robert, 94, 98, 124
bruises, 14

C
cakes and wine, 126
candle, 39, 62–64, 136
CASE system, 69, 70
casting, 151–152, 186
cauldron, 60
center, 5–6, 103, 105, 126,
    130–131, 133–136, 148, 151
ceremonial magick, xiv–xv, 58,
    85, 150, 152, 167
chakras, 63, 103–105, 108, 130,
    135, 142–143
chalice, 60
channeling, 38, 49–50, 103–
    104, 107, 125, 131, 143, 155,
    157, 160
chanting, 89–91, 107
chi, 7, 20, 37–39, 49–50, 64, 91,
    95, 98–101, 103, 107, 118,
    125, 128, 133, 148
Chi Kung, 37, 92, 100–101,
    104, 126, 134
choking, 15
choice, 31, 59, 112
Circle, 59, 61–63, 71, 85, 101,
    132, 146, 150–155, 168,
    177–178
clairvoyance, 130
Clauser, John, 79
closing, 41, 70, 131, 135, 143, 154
cognition, 20, 23, 92, 144
collapse, 37, 55–56, 81, 85, 101,
    107, 120, 148, 154
color, 62, 69–70, 137, 146

concentration, 6, 9, 34, 40, 50,
    52, 93, 118, 124, 141, 157,
    167, 177–178
cone of power, xiii
connection, xiv–xv, 4, 24,
    79, 83–84, 87–88, 95, 121,
    152–153, 177
consciousness, 8, 15, 20, 22–23,
    32, 35, 40, 53–54, 71, 74,
    84, 89, 93, 106, 111–112,
    116–117, 127, 131, 141, 144,
    156, 181
cord cutting, 158
courage, 26, 36
coven, 71
creativity, 69, 74, 93, 165
crystals, xiv, 36, 58, 72, 108, 120,
    177
cutting a doorway (magickal
    technique), 153
cutting links, 158

D
Dalibard, Jean, 79
dance, 10, 107
dantian, 101, 104, 142–143,
    148
death, 2, 7, 46, 117
deception, 31
decisions, 22, 57, 112, 166
decisiveness, 56
defense, xiv–xv, xvii, 2–5, 8–9,
    13, 15, 19, 24, 29, 33, 35, 44,
    46–47, 51–52, 56, 58–59, 61,
    63–64, 69–70, 72–74, 86,
    94–95, 99–100, 102–103, 109,
    119, 124–127, 130, 132–133,
    137, 140–146, 148, 150–153,

LLEWELLYN ORDERING INFORMATION

Order Online:
Visit our website at www.llewellyn.com, select your books, and order them on our secure server.

Order by Phone:
- Call toll-free within the U.S. at 1-877-NEW-WRLD (1-877-639-9753). Call toll-free within Canada at 1-866-NEW-WRLD (1-866-639-9753)
- We accept VISA, MasterCard, and American Express

Order by Mail:
Send the full price of your order (MN residents add 7% sales tax) in U.S. funds, plus postage & handling to:

> Llewellyn Worldwide
> 2143 Wooddale Drive, Dept. 978-0-7387-1219-2
> Woodbury, MN 55125-2989, U.S.A.

Postage & Handling:

Standard (U.S., Mexico, & Canada). If your order is:
> $24.99 and under, add $3.00
> $25.00 and over, FREE STANDARD SHIPPING

AK, HI, PR: $15.00 for one book plus $1.00 for each additional book.

International orders (airmail only):
> $16.00 for one book plus $3.00 for each additional book

Orders are processed within 2 business days.
Please allow for normal shipping time. Postage and handling rates subject to change.

Full Contact Magick

A Book of Shadows for the Wiccan Warrior

KERR CUHULAIN

Incorporate the Warrior archetype to access and use your magickal energy! Link the archetype of the Warrior to the archetype of the Magician. Instead of ready-made spells, this book gives you the foundation to take control of your own destiny. You will learn to access your internal energy and strength to overcome obstacles and problems in your life, to heal yourself mentally and emotionally, and to access your natural gifts. You will learn how to raise and direct magickal energy, create spells of your own, and create your own personal Book of Shadows, full of practical magickal techniques.

978-0-7387-0254-4
288 pages

$15.95

Instant Magick

Ancient Wisdom, Modern Spellcraft

CHRISTOPHER PENCZAK

What if you could practice magick anytime, without the use of ceremonial spells, altars, or magickal tools? Items such as candles, special ingredients, and exotic symbols are necessary to perform many types of magick, but these items aren't always feasible, attainable, or even available. The purest form of magick—tapping into your own energetic awareness to create change—is accessible simply through the power of your will.

By inspiring readers to explore their own individual willpower, popular author Christopher Penczak explains how to weave natural energies into every facet of life. This book features personalized techniques used to weed out any unwanted, unhealthy, or unnecessary desires to find a true, balanced magickal being. Penczak's innovative, modern spellcasting techniques utilize meditation, visualization, words, and intent in any situation, at any time. The results can seem instantaneous, and the potential limitless.

Christopher Penczak is a faculty member of the Northeast Institute of Whole Health (NEIWH) in Manchester, New Hampshire. He also teaches classes throughout New England on Witchcraft, meditation, Reiki, crystals, and shamanic journeys.

978-0-7387-0859-1
216 pages

$12.95

Sons of the Goddess

A Young Man's Guide to Wicca

CHRISTOPHER PENCZAK

This is Wicca 101 for young men. Wicca is a spiritual path open to all. Yet young men may have trouble identifying their place in this seemingly female-dominated religion. Without many male role models, how can one become empowered as a son of the Goddess?

Christopher Penczak, who learned about Witchcraft and magick in his late teens, offers guidance to all the young men out there who are curious about Wicca. This much-needed masculine perspective on the Craft discusses divine masculinity found in ancient myths, male energies, and rites of passage. Penczak also describes the fundamentals of Wicca, including the Rule of Three, the Wiccan Rede, spellcraft, rituals, holidays, and Witchcraft ethics.

978-0-7387-0547-7

216 pages

$15.95

To order, call 1-877-NEW-WRLD

Prices subject to change without notice

Coven Craft

Witchcraft for Three or More

Amber K

Here is the complete guidebook for anyone who desires to practice Witchcraft in a caring, challenging, well-organized spiritual support group: a coven. This book is for you whether you hope to learn more about this ancient spiritual path, are a coven member wanting more rewarding experiences in your group, are looking for a coven to join or are thinking of starting one, or you are a Wiccan elder gathering proven techniques and fresh ideas.

Amber K shares what she as learned in her twenty years as a Wiccan priestess about beginning and maintaining healthy covens. Learn what a coven is, how it works, and how you can make your coven experience more effective, enjoyable, and rewarding. Plus, get practical hands-on guidance in the form of sample Articles of Incorporation, Internet resources, sample by-laws, and sample budgets. Seventeen ritual scripts are also provided.

978-1-5671-8018-3
528 pages

$19.95

True Magick

A Beginner's Guide

AMBER K

True magick can change your life. With magick's aid, you can have vibrant health, prosperity, or a new career. You can enhance your relationships or bring new ones into your life. With magick, you can reach deep inside yourself to find confidence, courage, tranquility, faith, compassion, understanding, or humor. If you're curious about magick, you will find answers in this book. Amber K, a High Priestess of the Wiccan religion and an experienced practitioner of magick, explains not only the history and lore of magick, but also its major varieties in the world today. And if you want to practice magick, then this book will start you on the Path.

978-0-7387-0823-2
360 pages

$12.95

Llewellyn's 2008 Witches' Companion
An Almanac for Everyday Living

Irreverent, useful, and eclectic, Llewellyn's annual *Witches' Companion* will spark the interest of every Witch.

From craft essentials to holistic Witchery, this year's edition is filled with wry and relevant articles. Innovative thinkers, authors, and experts share personal and inspiring insights into a broad range of timely topics. Stay up-to-date on current debates in the Witch community. Revitalize your daily practice with fresh ideas in spellcraft. Discover what you can do to make your home the ultimate Earth-friendy abode. You'll also find thoughtful essays devoted to health and wellness, communication, and life transformation.

Also featured is a monthly calendar of correspondences and lunar information to fuel your magical workings.

978-0-7387-0560-6
288 pages

$9.99

The Complete Magician's Tables

STEPHEN SKINNER

Anyone practicing magic won't want to miss this comprehensive book of magician's correspondences. Featuring four times more tables than Aleister Crowley's *Liber 777*, this is the most complete collection of magician's tables available. This monumental work documents thousands of mystical links—spanning pagan pantheons, Kabbalah, astrology, tarot, I Ching, angels, demons, herbs, perfumes, and more!

The sources of this remarkable compilation range from classic grimoires such as the Sworn Book to modern theories of prime numbers and atomic weights. Data from Peter de Abano, Abbott Trithemius, Albertus Magnus, Cornelius Agrippa, and other prominent scholars is referenced here, in addition to hidden gems found in unpublished medieval grimoires and Kabbalistic works.

Well-organized and easy to use, *The Complete Magician's Tables* can help you understand the vast connections making up our strange and mysterious universe.

978-0-7387-1164-5
432 pages

$44.95